Do your relationships produce bondage or joy?

Breaking Unhealthy Soul-Ties

by Bill and Sue Banks

D1301483

Breaking Unhealthy Soul-Ties
by Bill and Sue Banks
ISBN 10: 0-89228-139-1
ISBN 13: 978-089228-139-8

Copyright © 1999, 2011
Impact Christian Books

Impact Christian Books, Inc.
332 Leffingwell Ave., Suite 101
Kirkwood, MO 63122

www.impactchristianbooks.com

February 1999	First Printing
March 2001	Second Printing
February 2003	Third Printing
July 2004	Fourth Printing
March 2006	Fifth Printing
January 2011	Sixth Printing

All passages are from the KING JAMES BIBLE unless otherwise noted.

Printed in the United States of America

CONTENTS

Foreword

Unhealthy soul-ties inevitably become demonic soul-ties. Having recognized the existence of demonic soul-ties, and having, through countless deliverance situations, confronted the spirits involved, it thrilled me to read this insightful, biblical treatise on the subject. It is a methodical discussion of the facts and principles involved in both good and bad soul-ties.

This book deals with a facet of deliverance that should never be neglected. Unhealthy soul-ties are the underlying cause for many disturbed lives. Unholy ties result from perverted and ungodly relationships which hinder believers in their spiritual walk and keep them bound in spiritual chains.

Here, at last, is a thorough and theologically sound treatment of a little understood subject. Here, too, is an opportunity to inventory one's own life as to the existence of unhealthy soul-ties, and to discover the necessary steps for breaking free into the purity and peace of deliverance.

Frank D. Hammond
(Minister and author of *Pigs in the Parlor,* and numerous other books.)

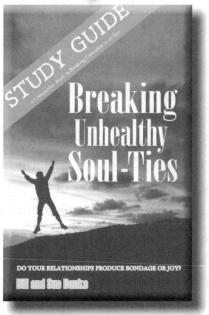

ISBN 089228031X

Study Guide: Breaking Unhealthy Soul-Ties
by Bill & Sue Banks

This Study Guide is a tool that can be used to diagnose and address the soul-ties in your life.

We all form ties with the people in our lives. Some of these ties are healthy, even God-inspired. Some, however, are unhealthy and demonically-inspired.

This companion book provides detail into what the soul is, how it functions, and how it can be affected by both positive and negative ties.

Impact Christian Books
www.impactchristianbooks.com
1-800-451-2708

Author's Preface

Part of the "trigger" for the study behind this book came from the closing passage in a letter that I received from Judson Cornwell in which he asked, "Is it possible that God is knitting our souls together?"

What a beautiful thought and yet that is exactly what I have come to discover should be the nature of the relationship existing between all believers. His statement started me thinking about positive soul-ties, which was basically a new area of thought

It also struck me that although we have heard a great deal in recent years concerning problems resulting from negative or evil soul-ties, I could not recall hearing that term even in deliverance circles prior to about 1980. I wondered how it was possible to suddenly be seeing so much truth regarding soul-ties if it hadn't been seen before. So I asked several other men who have distinguished themselves in the ministry of deliverance. They agreed that they too had never heard the term used earlier than about fifteen years ago.

Perhaps it took me twenty-eight years of ministering to those with needs for deliverance to be open and willing to understand soul-ties. I must confess that I had virtually no light on the subject at all until about the last five years. Prior to that time when I encountered them, I probably lumped them all under the general heading of witchcraft control and simply broke them. It is important to note that the Lord seems to be willing to honor the power of the Name of Jesus and of the Blood which He shed, even when we don't have a full and complete understanding of all the ways in which Satan operates.

The hour is soon coming when there will no longer be a need for anything to be kept secret... because the fullness of time is rapidly approaching.

> For nothing is secret, that shall not be made manifest; neither any thing hid, that shall not be known and come abroad.
>
> Luke 8:17

> What I tell you in darkness, that speak ye in light: and what ye hear in the ear, that preach ye upon the housetops.
>
> Matt. 10:27

Today, the Holy Spirit is training the Body of Christ and enhancing our discernment. It is apparent to me that mysteries of the Kingdom are being revealed in this hour, in order that the Body of Christ might be edified; that we might grow up unto Him – and into the full stature of the measure of Christ.

As with anything that is new or revelational, I urge you to read carefully, prayerfully, and cautiously with your own discernment on alert, for I am merely a seeker of truth, as you are: seeking answers to help *set the captives free*!

Bill Banks
Kirkwood, Missouri
January 1999

Introduction

While ministering in the field of deliverance from demonic bondage over the past twenty-eight years, we have discovered many truths concerning the enemy's plans and wiles for God's children. However, in recent years we have come to realize that there is a root problem underlying most demonic bondage. We describe such a root as an *unhealthy* or *ungodly* soul-tie.

A silly question often posed to theology students is: "Can God make a rock so large, He cannot lift it?" A ridiculous question. Why would God want to do such a thing? However, in essence, He has done so — in the form of freewill which He has granted to man.

☞ God created us with "freewill," (i.e., granted sovereignty to our wills). He has allowed us to make the decision as to whom we shall serve. He does not overpower our wills. Rather, He patiently waits for us to choose to bring our minds into complete allegiance to His will.

Given this fact, we are presented with free will — the most powerful force in God's creation. Its true power lies in God's refusal to either control it, or override it. The angels have free will; man, God's highest creation on this planet, has it; even the Godhead possesses it, as Jesus indicated:

> "My food... is to do the will of him who sent me"
> John 4:34a NIV

> Nevertheless not my will, but thine, be done.
>
> Luke 22:42b

In certain circumstances, when one submits his will to another, incredible good or demonic evil can occur.

We will attempt to define both sides of this issue: not only the benefits of Godly soul-ties, but also, the destructiveness of the ungodly ones.

We will further attempt to offer solutions to those people experiencing pain and demonic torment due to the existence of unhealthy adult soul-links.

The remedy for deliverance from evil spirits is relatively simple by comparison with the breaking of evil soul-ties: one can readily cast out a demon, but how does one cast out a person exerting influence in his life? A person who is usually a mixture of good and evil?

It is not by accident that Jesus commanded us to forgive before we were to be delivered (as in the Lord's Prayer) because He recognized that demonic bondages often stem from broken relationships of trust between people.

> And forgive us our debts, **as we forgive** our debtors. And
> lead us not into temptation, but **deliver us** from evil...
>
> Matt. 6:12–13a

Just as no two snowflakes are alike, so no two relationships are identical. However, there can be common characteristics evidenced both in beneficial and unhealthy soul-ties.

It is our hope that by assisting the reader in clarifying both the positive and negative aspects of relationships, he or she will gain greater spiritual freedom and maturity.

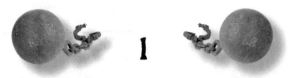

1
THE SOUL
AND ITS FUNCTION

MAN AS TRIUNE

Man was made in the image and likeness of God his Creator. God is Trinity: a three-in-one being.

Starting with the very basics, man, made like his God, also is a triune being. He is a **spirit**, he has a **soul**, and both of these are clothed (or housed) in a **body of flesh**. The spirit and soul of the regenerate (born again) man will one day depart from his earthly house, called a tent, or tabernacle in Scripture, and enter a heavenly one, as the Apostle Peter said of himself: (1 Pet. 1:4; 2 Pet. 1:13,14)

> ...shortly I must put off this my tabernacle.
>
> 2 Pet. 1:14

Dennis Bennett, who seemed to exude more love than any man I've ever met, and who was trained as a theologian, expressed the concept of the trinity of man to me in the form of an 'H' diagram. (See figure on next page.)

Spirit — The spirit is the Divine (God) Nature of man designed to be in regular communication with God.

Soul — The soul is the mind, the intellect, the will, the emotions, the choice or decision-making part of man - specifically his personality. It is that part of man which enables him to live in this world (language, math, social skills, etc.).

Body — The body is the house in which the other two live, and provides the means whereby the other two express themselves.

Your soul is the *real you*. As an example, if you were to lose the use of your arms and legs, thus preventing you from doing or going; if you were also to lose your sight, your hearing, and the use of your tongue, you would be incapable of expressing yourself, but *you* would still exist. You would still be the same person, but you would be unable to express your *personality*.

In a normal situation your personality expresses itself through your body. In an ideal situation, as represented in the Bennett diagram, your spirit is fully attuned to God, and guides your soul, which in turn directs your body.

We are permitted to see an instance of this proper functioning of spirit-soul-body in the beautiful passage from Psalm 103. In it we find *the spirit* of David addressing and instructing *the soul* of David to properly respond to the Lord by means of his physical *body* (in this case, his tongue).

> **Bless the LORD, O my soul**: and all that is within me, bless his holy name. Bless the LORD, O my soul, and forget not all his benefits: Who forgiveth all thine iniquities; who healeth all thy diseases.
>
> Ps. 103:1–3

The soul of man, as indicated, is that part of man which is uniquely him. It is what we think of as the personality of the man. We learn the nature and character of a man by observing the expression of his soul through both his words and his actions. These originate in his soul. The Scripture reveals that the soul of man is composed of the mind (intellect), the will and the emotions (and desires).

Mind – the intellect, a capacity to know.

> ...marvellous are thy works; and that my **soul knoweth** right well. Ps. 139:14

> Also, that the **soul be without knowledge**, it is not good... Prov. 19:2a

Will – the capacity to exercise choice, make decisions, and push one towards self-preservation, self-control.

> And it shall come to pass, that **every soul, which will not hear**... shall be destroyed Acts 3:23

> ...nevertheless **not my will**, but thine, be done. Luke 22:42

Emotions – the capacity to feel, to experience.

> ...my **soul is cast down** within me... Ps. 42:6a

> Tell me, O thou whom **my soul loveth**... Song 1:7a

> My **soul is exceeding sorrowful**... Matt. 26:38a

> And my **soul shall be joyful**...shall rejoice in his salvation. Ps. 35:9

Desires – surprisingly, souls may desire and even lust.

> Delight thyself also in the LORD; and he shall give thee the **desires** of thine heart. Ps. 37:4

> ...whatsoever thy **soul lusteth after**. Deut. 12:20b

> And the fruits that thy **soul lusted** after are departed from thee... Rev. 18:14a

The spirit-man is intended to have dominion, to rule over, the natural or carnal man. The dysfunctional soul is carnal. In Scripture carnality refers to everything in man that is not under the control, or dominion of the Holy Spirit, via your own yielded spirit. The proper soul is a submitted will, intellect and emotional being. In Romans chapters seven and eight, Paul illustrates the problems of the carnal man, and the gloriously victorious walk awaiting the man whose Holy Spirit governed spirit rules in his soul and body.

> For the good that I would I do not: but the evil which I would not, that I do.
>
> Rom. 7:19

> For they that are after the flesh do mind the things of the flesh; but they that are after the Spirit the things of the Spirit. For to be carnally minded is death; but to be spiritually minded is life and peace.
>
> Rom. 8:6

In a broad sense, *godly soul-ties* are those formed within or around a godly context (or centered in God); *ungodly* are those formed outside a godly context, or even against godly admonitions (such as those with a harlot). Soul-ties are rather difficult to define, in that there may be as many different variations as there are people, and any given individual may be under pressure from several of varying degrees at the same time. So the best we can do is to give a broad generic definition and then attempt to increase our understanding and to amplify our definition as we consider illustrations of the specific types of soul-ties.

WHAT IS A SOUL-TIE?

A soul-tie is a *cleaving together*, a relationship whereby two souls are joined or knitted together, and in a sense become as one.

In the Scripture, "cleave" means to be "knit together," "bound up," or to "cleave together."

ے *Strong's Exhaustive Concordance Dictionary* defines "cleave," (#1692, *dabaq*, pronounced daw-bak) as "to cling or adhere; (figuratively) to catch by pursuit: to abide, cleave, to follow hard after, be joined together, overtake, pursue hard, stick, take."

Thus, to be linked to another person by means of a soul-tie, is to *cling to,* or to be *closely attached* to, that person. It is as if one were stuck or glued to them, as being lovingly devoted to someone.

A soul-tie is a means whereby a person is brought into a relationship and becomes one (one flesh, one-mind or one-soul) with another human being. Some refer to this phenomenon, as is done in the field of psychology, as "mind control," "mind-links" or "soul-links," but we will continue to use the terms "godly" and "ungodly" soul-ties to describe and distinguish between those which are godly and beneficial and those which are detrimental to the well-being of the ones so united.

The word *tie* is defined by Webster as meaning "to attach, bind, fasten; a bond of kinship or affection, as to unite in marriage." However, the definition also carries another connotation: **"to restrain from independence or freedom of action or choice: constrain by, or as if by authority, influence,**

agreement or obligation." The individual being so controlled feels obliged, and as if his independence must be sacrificed due to the influence or authority of the other party, who is controlling. An extreme example of this negative kind of soul-tie may be seen in many of those individuals in Germany during WWII, who were coerced to do things against their nature, due to the influence of Hitler and Nazi peer pressure.

How is it that Soul-Ties Exist?

Soul-ties exist because God wanted close godly bonds, or soul-ties, between His people. Soul-ties are God-designed and were intended for man's best interests. We can see that soul-ties were in God's plan from the very beginning. God chose to begin His earthly work with an exclusive, walking, talking relationship with His son, Adam.

There should be a two-way flow of love between the linked parties; love should flow in both directions in a healthy, Godly soul-tie. This thought is advanced in the *Umbilical Concept* which follows and is seen to relate both to Godly soul-ties or godly bonds, and also later to ungodly.

Involuntary to Voluntary Attachment
The Umbilical Concept

In human reproduction, the mother-to-be is vitally linked to her unborn child via the connection which exists through the umbilical cord. The child draws sustenance, nourishment and life through that vital union with the earthly source of his natural life. This is a vertical umbilical relationship which provides us life, and it is *involuntary* on the child's part.

17

Initially, the child is totally dependent upon the mother for life, blood, oxygen, nourishment. On the subtler, less obvious side, she passes on to the child the DNA that will direct his growth, determine his hair color, eye color, height, body type, and many other factors that will affect his personality. Oftentimes the mother also passes down curses or spirits, such as alcoholism, drug addiction, or fears. All information passes to the developing child through the umbilical cord and is carried by the blood.

Outside the womb, as time passes, attachment becomes *voluntary* and such links continue primarily as a matter of choice. In adults, relationships are voluntarily interdependent based upon trust, confidence, or love.

THREE MAIN CATEGORIES
OF SOUL-TIES

There can be *intellectual* or "platonic" soul-ties of the mind, such as those formed between student and teacher, or disciple and mentor. These would normally be neutral, unless the one who has voluntarily placed himself "under the other's tutelage" begins to be unable to assert his own will. Platonic ties are often dissolved and outgrown, when the teacher-student role is completed, or may fairly easily be broken once recognized. However, these relationships can progress from that of simple student-teacher, to dependence and bondage to the teacher and even into idolatry. Such relationships usually begin based upon shared ideas, beliefs, concepts, understandings or goals.

Soul-ties that exist on an *emotional* level are based on emotional attachments such as common feelings of love, fear or hatred. The bonds of family are included, such as the soul-ties

18

between husband and wife or parent and child. Also included are the bonds of friendship. When imbalanced, these healthy soul-ties can become distorted or perverted.

Erotic or physical love attachments are soul-ties formed by ③ sin. Bonds are formed in sinful sexual encounters such as rape, molestation or incest. Any kind of illicit sex, such as adultery and harlotry, form ties between the participating parties.

Soul-ties do not usually form overnight, (except in the case of soul-ties based upon commission of sin, as that with the harlot).

☞ Usually soul-ties are formed over a period of time, as a result of numerous decisions to submit to another person.

There is a Jewish tradition that Jacob illustrated the power of unity to his sons by taking twelve sticks (one for each of his sons) and tying them in a bundle. He then asked each of his sons to attempt to break the bundle. None was able. Afterwards he removed the individual sticks and gave each to a son who could easily snap it.

JESUS OUR PATTERN

Jesus was the only man who ever lived in a sinless body, and who possessed an undamaged soul. Jesus led a happy, spiritually successful life because He knew the following truths, which He also taught:

> For whosoever will save his life shall lose it; but whosoever shall lose his life for my sake and the gospel's, the same shall save it.
>
> Mark 8:35

...the prince of this world cometh, hath nothing in me.

John 14:30

All human soul-ties must be counterbalanced by a love for Jesus.

He that loveth father or mother more than me is not worthy of me: and he that loveth son or daughter more than me is not worthy of me.

Matt. 10:34–37

Jesus, obviously, is not speaking in this passage of a man actually hating his father, for that contradicts the sense of the overall teachings of Jesus. He is teaching that *relatively*, a man's love for Jesus must be so much greater than that for his own father, as to make the natural love seem less. He also warns that love for Jesus and the seeking of His kingdom will often prove to be divisive and may be misunderstood by men.

The way we avoid loving man too much, or becoming too attached (bound) to any man, is by loving Jesus more. Also, we have seen the necessity of walking in truth. To make any compromise with truth is dangerous. There is no such thing as a "little" or "white" lie. It is still a lie, big or small, and thus is a denial of the truth. Any relinquishment to something less than the truth is to identify oneself with untruth, and is tantamount to identifying with Satan and his kingdom, for Jesus identified Himself as the Truth:

I am the way, the **truth**, and the life: no man cometh unto the Father, but by me.

John 14:6

TRUTH MUST NOT BE COMPROMISED

Paul and John warned against compromise both by their actions and by their words:

> This matter arose because some false believers had infiltrated our ranks to spy on the freedom we have in Christ Jesus and to **make us slaves**. We did not give in to them for a moment, so that the truth of the gospel might be preserved for you.
>
> Gal. 2:4-5 NIV

> If anyone comes to you and does not bring this teaching, do not receive him into your house, and do not give him a greeting; for the one who gives him a greeting participates in his evil deeds.
>
> 2 John 1:10 -11 NASB

When Jesus spoke of Himself as *the Truth*, the word He chose in the Greek literally means *reality*. "I am the reality," He was saying, which truth of course is. An alternative to the problem of negative soul-ties is the hope of the new relationships which Jesus introduced:

> And he answered them, saying, Who is my mother, or my brethren? ... and said, Behold my mother and my brethren! For whosoever shall do the will of God, the same is my brother, and my sister, and mother.
>
> Mark 3:33-35

Jesus made a decision to be controlled only by God, and no one else, even those whom He greatly loved. We must do the same, determining not to allow even loving relationships to draw us into a state of disobedience to God. Anything less than full, total and immediate obedience, is disobedience.

OUR PATTERN REFUSED BONDAGE

Jesus refused the bondage of those closest to Him, namely, His mother. When His mother tried to get Him to manifest His miracle-working power before He was ready, he responded,

> Woman, what have I to do with thee? Mine hour is not yet come.
>
> John 2:4

Jesus refused to move ahead of God's timetable, and to do anything for any selfish benefit. He was awaiting the go-ahead from His heavenly Father to work the great prophetic miracle at Cana which would launch His supernatural miracle, ministry of obedience. He resisted every ungodly pressure, whether to work miracles outside of God's timing (Matt. 4:3) for the wrong reasons (Matt. 4:6), to submit to someone other than the Father (Matt. 4:9) or to prove Himself to man (John 3:18, 6:30).

He also resisted the pressure placed upon Him by His own brothers. He resisted the temptation to please man; the man-pleasing spirit was rejected. He refused to come under their influence. The definition of demonization is to be under the influence of an ungodly spirit.

> Jesus' brothers said to him, "Leave Galilee and go to Judea, so that your disciples there may see the works you do. No one who wants to become a public figure acts in secret... show yourself to the world." For even his own brothers did not believe in him. Therefore Jesus told them, "My time is not yet here; for you any time will do."
>
> John 7:3–6 NIV

Jesus refused to be deterred from God's plans for His life by Satan speaking through one of His closest and most intimate friends, Peter, a member of His inner circle. Jesus was explaining the nature of the death that he would soon experience in Jerusalem, when Peter began to rebuke Him, saying,

> Peter took him aside and began to rebuke him. "Never, Lord!" he said. "This shall never happen to you!"
>
> Matt. 16:22 NIV

Jesus then rebuked the words which Satan had spoken to Him through the mouth of His dear friend.

> ...he rebuked Peter. "Get behind me, Satan!" he said. "You do not have in mind the concerns of God, but merely human concerns.
>
> Mark 8:33 NIV

Luke adds a significant additional clause.

> And Jesus answered and said unto him, Get thee behind me, Satan: for it is written, Thou shalt worship the Lord thy God, and **him only shalt thou serve**.
>
> Luke 4:8

Satan was attempting to deflect Jesus from the will of God, trying to appeal to His own flesh which stood in opposition to the will of God. Luke points out in the preceding passage that it is God *alone* whom we should serve. In other words we are again admonished *to be in subjection to no man, but only unto God*; to serve God and Him alone, faithfully and without reservation, without being bound by unbalanced soul-ties to any man.

Jesus resisted the temptation of seeking public approval. He sought not the approval of man, only the approval of His heavenly Father and the doing of His will. He did not need, seek, nor accept the world's approval, which could easily have been His. He knew that in man was the tendency to control, to use, or to depend upon Him naturally instead of supernaturally.

> Now in Jerusalem at the passover... many believed... when they saw the miracles which he did. **But Jesus did not commit himself unto them, because he knew all men**... for he knew what was in man.
>
> John 2:22–25

Satan also attempted to establish an attachment, a source of control with Jesus on the Mount of Temptation when he sought the obedience and worship of Christ. Thus we see the strength that Jesus manifested in His single-minded commitment to placing God, His Father, first.

Jesus even refused to assert His own soul's need for self-preservation, as evidenced when He prayed thrice in the Garden to bring His flesh into submission to His Spirit, which was already in obedience unto the will of God. Thus, He prayed,

> Saying, Father, if thou be willing, remove this cup from me: nevertheless **not my will**, but thine, be done.
>
> Luke 22:42

Clearly the will of God was in conflict with his own will (soul), which is why he prayed so fervently to bring His soul under the domination of His spirit.

God Wants Unhealthy Soul-Ties Broken

God desires to restore our souls that we might be able to seek Him with our whole (entire) spirit, soul and body.

> And the very God of peace sanctify you wholly; and I pray to God your **whole spirit** and **soul** and **body** be preserved blameless unto the coming of our Lord Jesus Christ.
>
> 1 Thes. 5:23

☞ We cannot be obedient to God's command to serve Him with all of our soul, if we lack possession of a complete, whole soul!

> But take diligent heed to do the commandment and the law, which Moses the servant of the LORD charged you, to love the LORD your God, and to walk in all his ways, and to keep his commandments, and to cleave unto him, and to serve him with **all your heart and with all your soul**.
>
> Josh. 22:5

Therefore, it seems evident that in order to be able to love God with "all one's soul," we should better understand godly and ungodly soul-ties, which are explored in the following chapter.

2

SOUL-TIES:
GODLY AND UNGODLY

Perhaps it would be helpful at the outset to differentiate between godly soul-ties and ungodly soul-ties. Remember, a soul-tie is a bonding in the soulish realm; a bonding between the souls of two or more people. Although in today's thinking any links to another person are generally thought to be unhealthy, there are *healthy* and Godly soul-ties. The first soul-tie was designed by God and intended for the benefit of the first couple.

All soul-ties incorporate influence, compromise and obedience for the sake of peaceful coexistence. Godly soul-ties have a settling, peaceful influence and not only help to stabilize the relationship with another, but also with the Heavenly Father. I believe far more godly soul-ties exist than ungodly.

In an ungodly soul-tie, one individual pulls another away from his or her commitment to God's laws of morality and obedience. We think of such pulls as evil soul-ties, wherein the one who becomes linked with another person finds himself to be corrupted by the association. Paul warns against these types of relationships in 1 Corinthians:

> Do not be deceived: "Bad company corrupts good morals."
> 1 Cor. 15:33 NASB

The literal meaning of this passage might be rendered, *do not let depraved companionship spoil or defile your moral habits* (i.e. your manner or acting).

Consider the godly soul-ties outlined in Scripture. God saw that man was incomplete alone. He was made for union. First and foremost, man was designed for union with Christ, for without God a void exists. Secondly, man was designed for union with his wife — his helpmate. Finally, man was designed for union with his fellow man.

> Love thy neighbour as thyself.   Lev. 19:18

Our first and primary soul-tie is therefore union with Christ. That is, be yoked with God.

> Take **my yoke** upon you, and learn of me; for I am meek
> and lowly in heart: and ye shall find rest unto your souls.
> Matt. 11:29

ನ In this passage, the Greek word for yoke is *zugos*. In Strong's, *zugos* (#2218), pronounced dzoo-gos, is from the root of zeugnumi (to join, especially by a yoke); it represents a coupling, i.e. (figuratively) servitude through law or obligation; (literally) a pair of balances, yoke.

Christ calls His people into vital union with Him. In addition to the figure of the yoke, He also figuratively uses the connection of the branches to the vine as the means for the believers to draw sustenance and produce fruit.

We are called upon to be in vital union with Christ in a variety of metaphors and similes, such as being united with Him, the Bread from heaven, by which we are to sustain ourselves; as the Vine to which we are attached as branches; as the Head to which we are attached as members of His Body; as the Shepherd whose flock we are; a King and Lord whose subjects we are; and as the Bridegroom for whom we await as the Bride. We, as His Body, are called to be one; to exist in union with Him, and in unity with one another.

There is a Scriptural confirmation of the Umbilical Concept in his teaching regarding the vine.

CHRIST'S VINE ANALOGY
IS THE UMBILICAL CONCEPT

Jesus' illustration of the vine explains how the Body should function and relate to Him. He is explaining that we should be vitally dependent upon Him for all things.

> **I am the true vine**, and my Father is the husbandman. Abide in me, and I in you. As the branch cannot bear fruit of itself, except it abide in the vine; no more can ye, except ye abide in me. I am the vine, ye are the branches: He that abideth in me, and I in him, the same bringeth forth much fruit: for without me ye can do nothing.
>
> John 15:1,4–5

We are only able to bear fruit by depending upon Him, by

drawing strength and our very life from Him. Our own strength and effort in the flesh will not have life-changing impact upon the lives of others; it is only as we allow His life to be manifested through us, as we allow ourselves to be His agents, or branches, enabling His love to flow outward, that fruit is produced in the lives of others.

From the vine the branch receives:

Nourishment – We are fed spiritually by staying in union with Him; like the little birds in the nest we simply open our mouths in faith expecting Him to provide life-giving sustenance to us. We thus are able to feed on the Word of God, just as Jesus taught.

God desires to be our Source! He feeds us with the real sustenance of life — every word that proceeds out of the mouth of God.

Now the just **shall live** by faith...   Heb. 10:38a

Growth – We grow up spiritually as we choose to draw upon Him as our source of life and nourishment, and to feed upon His Word.

As newborn babes, desire the sincere milk of the word, that ye **may grow** thereby...
1 Pet. 2:2

But speaking the truth in love, [that you] may **grow up** into him in all things, which is the head, even Christ...
Eph. 4:15

> But **grow in grace**, and in the knowledge of our Lord and Saviour Jesus Christ.
>
> 2 Pet. 3:18a

Both the potential for growth and the very DNA of the vine is passed to the branches as the vital contact is maintained so that each will possess the same characteristics and nature as the vine upon which they develop.

Support and strength – The vine provides the support that prevents the branch from sagging down into the corruption of the earth and being destroyed by long-term contact. The uplifting force of the vine aids the branches, keeping them off the ground, and the pattern of its strength encourages us to...

> ...lay aside every weight, and the sin which doth so easily beset us...
>
> Heb. 12:1

It is also through the support and strength of Jesus Christ that the Body is built and maintained.

> From him the whole body, joined and held together by every supporting ligament, grows and builds itself up in love, as each part does its work.
>
> Eph. 4:16

Guidance – Just as the Vine "plans" and directs the growth of the branches to be exactly where they can be of the most benefit to the plant, so it is in the Kingdom.

Jesus deploys His workers where He wants them for the good of the Body and for the accomplishment of His purposes. He has a wonderful plan for the entire Body.

> After these things the Lord appointed other seventy also, and **sent them... into every city and place, whither he himself would come.**
>
> Luke 10:1

The vine causes a lifting up. The vine exerts an "upward-calling," urging the plant to grow higher and upward.

> And let us consider one another to provoke unto love and to good works...
>
> Heb. 10:24

Fruit-bearing – The purpose of the vine is that it might bear good fruit for the kingdom of God, and bring glory to God.

> For we are his workmanship, created in Christ Jesus unto **good works**, which God hath before ordained that we should walk in them.
>
> Eph. 2:10

> Let your light so shine before men, that they may see your **good works**, and glorify your Father which is in heaven.
>
> Matt. 5:16

> ...having heard the word, keep it, and **bring forth fruit** with patience.
>
> Luke 8:15

> Herein is my Father glorified, that ye **bear much fruit**; so shall ye be my disciples.
>
> John 15:8

Protection – The strength and support of the vine sustains the branches, and the interrelationship between the branches affords mutual protection from strong winds and storms, which increases the strength of the entire body of the plant or vine.

> Be watchful, and strengthen the things which remain, that are ready to die...
>
> Rev. 3:2a

> But I have prayed for thee, that thy faith fail not: and when thou art converted, strengthen thy brethren.
>
> Luke 22:32

Gift – the life of the Vine is a gift.

> For by grace are ye saved through faith; and that not of yourselves: it is the **gift of God.**
>
> Eph. 2:8

Body to Body Ministry – Staying connected to the Vine allows for life to flow horizontally, from one believer to another.

> Our hope is that, as your faith continues to grow, **our sphere of activity among you will greatly expand...**
>
> 2 Cor. 10:15b NIV

MAN AND THE CREATION

God wanted this world to be a visible representation of His invisible attributes, eternal power, and Divine nature.

> For since the creation of the world God's invisible qualities—his eternal power and divine nature—have been clearly seen, being understood from what has been made, so that people are without excuse.
>
> Rom. 1:20 NIV

All of God's creation is "very good" and was meant to give man provision and refreshment. Man, when he fully appreciates the beauty and intelligence of all things created as a representation of the beauty and intelligence of the Creator, will be able to form a healthy relationship with the world around him.

However, we are not to love the world, nor to become unduly attached to it; nor to things, even inanimate objects, so as to worship the creation rather than the Creator. There are curses attached to some objects. Soul-ties can be formed with objects through *sentimental attachment*; "I cannot part with it," "I can't live without it." Man can become so soul-bound to an animal that it takes precedence over human relationships. Attaching too much importance to things or to places allows such items to become idols for us.

> Love not the world, neither the things that are in the world. If any man love the world, the love of the Father is not in him.
>
> 1 John 2:15

The Greek word for love used in I John is *agapao*, to love

with the God kind of love, in a social or moral sense. Man, however, has perverted the love of God and replaced it with the love of the world, His creation. Man has formed a soul-tie with the *created* instead of the *Creator*.

> I say that the things which the Gentiles sacrifice, they sacrifice to demons and not to God; and I do not want you to become **sharers in demons**.
>
> 1 Cor. 10:20 NASB

> For if you ever go back and **cling to**... these nations... and intermarry with them, so that you associate with them and they with you, know with certainty that the LORD your God will not continue to drive these nations out from before you; but **they will be a snare and a trap to you**, and a whip on your sides and thorns in your eyes, **until you perish** from off this good land which the LORD your God has given you.
>
> Josh. 23:12–13 NASB

> Professing themselves to be wise, they became fools, And changed the glory of the uncorruptible God into an image made like to corruptible man, and to birds, and fourfooted beasts, and creeping things ... Who changed the truth of God into a lie, and **worshipped and served the creature more than the Creator**, who is blessed for ever. Amen.
>
> Rom. 1:22–25

This attachment opens the way for demonic invasion of a person's life. Matthew states that one cannot serve two masters (Matt. 6:24). To be linked to Christ means to view His creation as a revelation *of* the Creator.

It is possible for man to bind himself to demons by turning a created thing into an object of worship or by seeking protection from it, as in witchcraft. But for the purposes of this book we will limit ourselves primarily to those soul-ties which occur between two or more human beings and the potential for bondages to develop in those relationships.

UNION WITH SPOUSE AND FAMILY

In the marriage union, husband and wife become one flesh as seen in God's command to Adam and Eve:

> Therefore **shall a man leave** his father and his mother, and **shall cleave unto his wife**: and they shall be one flesh.
>
> Gen. 2:24

The first soul-tie was designed and intended for the first couple. In the first command or principle given to man regarding marriage, God required the man entering marriage to "leave" and "cleave." That is, he should break the emotional soul-ties and the control of his parents, replacing them with a godly soul-tie by cleaving to his wife. God speaks of making of two individuals into one new flesh, or one single individual. The visible memorial of this union is the child with which the union is blessed.

> So they are no longer two, but **one flesh**. What therefore God has joined together, let no man separate.
>
> Matt. 19:6 NASB

Because man's deepest emotions involve his feelings toward his mate, or potential mate, this is a primary area for soul-tie danger. Man has mistakenly relegated marriage to an agreement between two people, rather than a lifelong, God-ordained, covenant tie. Thus like many other arrangements between people, it has, in at least fifty-percent of the cases, become doomed to failure.

Man Incomplete by Design

Man was designed with a need for a helpmate. God knew from the planning stage that man was incomplete and said, *It is not good for the man to be alone. I will make a helper suitable for him* (Gen. 2:18). There exists in man, as created, a need for a relationship and the absence of that relationship leaves a void unless filled with God.

Marriage was originally intended, as seen in the case of Adam and Eve, to be a covenant agreement between two people of the opposite sex whom God had made for each other. The covenant was pronounced in Adam's own words:

> This is now bone of my bones, and flesh of my flesh: she shall be called Woman, because she was taken out of Man. Therefore shall a man leave his father and his mother, and **shall cleave unto his wife**: and they shall be **one flesh**.
>
> Gen. 2:23–24

Thus, by its nature, marriage existed with two dimensions: a horizontal dimension between the two parties and a vertical dimension in which they recognized themselves to be under, and indebted to, God for one another.

THE GODLY UNION UNDER ATTACK

It is both interesting and enlightening to observe that until there was a marriage, Satan didn't bother directing an attack upon Adam. As soon as there was a marriage, Satan attempted to destroy the first couple!

Parenthetically, it wasn't until the first godly soul-tie was established that Satan attempted to destroy the united participants. He obviously hates the enormous potential for good resident within a godly soul-tie.

Unfortunately Satan succeeded, and Adam succumbed to the disobedient suggestion (pressure) of his wife, rather than heeding the express Word of God. Satan caused Adam to come under the soulish influence of Eve by placing her wishes above God's direct command. This resulted not only in loss of residence in Eden, and curses on both their ensuing lives, but an overall corruption of all creation due to the entrance of death.

Soul-ties, which began as godly bonds formed in marriage, can become perverted, distorted and even broken. A godly soul-tie even in a Christian marriage can become damaged or broken as a result of infidelity, which leads to guilt, resentment, unforgiveness, bitterness, and finally very frequently, converts the last vestiges of love to hate.

A healthy marital soul-tie can be permanently damaged as a result of broken vows or promises, such as those to stop drinking or doing drugs. Such failures often produce disappointment, resentment, bitterness, unforgiveness and finally divorce. The wife may leave as a result of the husband's failure to quit drinking or doing drugs, but it can happen either way. The husband is most apt to blame himself for failures to live up to standards which he may have set for himself and the breaking of promises made, such as to have a house of their own within two years. This leads to guilt, often shifting the blame to the wife (for not cooperating, spending too much, etc.), and so he goes looking for solace in a bottle or with another woman.

Since Adam's time, even in God-ordained marriages there can be wrongful soul-ties or abusive control of one partner by the other. For example, there is the typical emasculated husband who is dominated by a woman and lives a henpecked existence, escaping into fantasy, unable to assert his true personality. There are those Jezebel-type cases where control is exerted by a strong-willed woman who attempts to control her husband's life. Finally, there are the opposite "he-man" types, who demand total acquiescence and subservience to their demands in order for them to feel truly masculine.

EVEN GOD-ORDAINED, COVENANT SOUL-TIES CAN BE BROKEN

Ungodly soul-ties can lead to the dissolution of marriage. A very common type of soul-tie which is involved in the breakup of marriages is that formed with another woman outside the marriage. Such soul-ties may be formed as the result of a physical, sexual union (as in I Cor. 6:16), or because of an emotional soul-tie which may or may not consciously start out with any type of dating or sexual overtones. These are often simply friendships which become something more.

The other woman initially either fills some sort of void, that of a mother figure, friend, companion, or workplace partner, or offers an easy escape from the necessary responsibilities and effort required to maintain a healthy marriage. In recent decades these problems have increased astronomically due to the epidemic of divorce and have placed so many divorced people (especially women) in the work place. Lonely people seek someone to alleviate their loneliness, and working together creates opportunities for many snares to be laid. Today there are many women who want to find a man at any cost, and many men devoid of moral standards.

The inability to break with *preexisting* ungodly soul-ties can also contribute to the breakup of marriages. The young man who cannot break free from "his mother's apron strings," as it is usually expressed, is a poor candidate for a strong or successful marriage. Some overcome this type of pressure by moving away which is usually a great help. I have counseled with several women whose husbands seemed to be unable to make any decisions without first consulting mother. Several have complained that his mother would demand (or expect) him to be at her house to take care of her needs and of her house, while the wife and children were neglected, and their own house fell into a state of disrepair.

The new husband who seems unable to grow up and face his responsibilities, and cannot break the soul-ties with his former evil or immature companions, is also a poor candidate for marriage. These men feel they have to go out every night with their male friends to bars, strip joints or other entertainment, and then cannot understand why they can't quit drinking, smoking or doing drugs, as they have promised themselves and their wives.

A successful young businessman of about twenty-eight came and received salvation and the Baptism in the Holy Spirit in our prayer room; later he came back for deliverance. He confessed that he was having a problem breaking free from smoking pot. He had a history of drug use during his previous career as a professional athlete but wanted to be completely clean for his marriage and to be able to honorably follow the Lord. He admitted that a part of his problem in staying free was that his best friend, another very successful businessman, was still actively smoking pot and offered him some every time they were together. He usually met his friend at least one night a week. He and his wife were praying for his victory, but he kept failing due to the pressure from his friends. This illustrates the truth of the Scripture previously mentioned:

> ...evil communications [associations, fellowship] corrupt good manners [good conduct, good intentions].
> 1 Cor. 15:33b [BRACKETS OURS]

Forgiveness and kindness strengthen the healthy marriage bond between two people. Furthermore, as Ecclesiastes points out, *a threefold cord is not quickly broken* (4:12). God hates divorce, and certainly a shared, active faith in Christ will knit the two partners firmly together, causing their house to remain standing even after storms have come.

FAMILY TIES, SUCH AS A FATHER AND SON

Judah describes a soul-tie between Jacob and Benjamin, spoken to Joseph before he revealed himself to his brethren:

> Now therefore when I come to thy servant my father, and the lad be not with us; seeing that **his life is bound up in the lad's life**...
> Gen. 44:30

Judah stated that the life of Jacob was "bound up" in that of his son. The meaning of this phrase is very similar to that of

41

cleave in the original Greek.

&❧ Strong's indicates that "bound up" in the passage above is *kaw-shar'* (#7194), and it means to tie (in love, league), to bind up, to join together, and to knit stronger.

These are the family ties that exist between parent and child, brother and brother, brother and sister, where "blood is thicker than water" (which is the world's commentary upon such God-ordained bonds), or "natural" bonding. God obviously intended for the parent-child relationship to be an earthly representation of His familial ties with us. We have been told that we are His children, His adopted sons.

> But as many as received him, to them gave he power to become the **sons of God**...
>
> John 1:12a

The same characteristics of obedience and love should be found in the children, and wise training tempered with sacrificial love in the parent(s).

Symptoms of ungodly bonds are those of the son who hates his father, or the daughter who hates her mother due either to over-control and domination, or to lack of any reasonable discipline. These obviously are perverted and unnatural feelings. A parent who can't or won't maintain his authority through proper discipline becomes bound to the dominion and control of the rebellious and demanding child.

There can likewise be idolatrous soul-ties of a parent-to-a-child. God helped Abraham deal with Isaac and that very issue at the altar. God intends that we love our children but does not want us to make idols of them. It is a matter of degree and of priorities. Similarly, sometimes there are idolatrous soul-ties of child-to-parent. Jesus wants to be first in our hearts and lives, as He said.

> He that loveth father or mother more than me is not worthy of me: and he that loveth son or daughter more than me is not worthy of me.
>
> Matt. 10:37

PRENATAL VULNERABILITY

If a child picks up parental demons of fear, addictions, or curses, then he becomes far more susceptible to unhealthy soul-ties after birth. The Scripture makes it clear that evil forces may come into play in a life while a child is still in the womb.

> The wicked are estranged from the womb: they go astray as soon as they be born, speaking lies.
>
> Ps. 58:3

Children with physical problems can easily become dominated by authority figures, unless the parent wisely encourages their independence.

POST-NATAL VULNERABILITY
(DISCIPLINE FAILURES & CONTROL ISSUES)

God's judgment came upon the priest Eli and his household because he failed to exercise his authority in restraining his sons.

...I will judge his house for ever for the iniquity which he knoweth; because his sons made themselves vile, and **he restrained them not.**

1 Sam. 3:13

Many parents today, like Eli, are too permissive with their children, and refuse to punish them from a fear of losing their love (especially after a divorce), from a fear of their rage or violence, or to compromise with the world (everyone else is doing it). The net effect is summed up in Scripture as a judgment of God upon the failure to discipline:

And I will give **children to be their princes,** and **babes shall rule over them.** As for my people, children are their oppressors, and women rule over them.

Isa. 3:4, 12a

Parents who yield to a child's manipulation soon come into a form of bondage to the child. We encountered a case where the child threw a tantrum and vomited when his parents attempted to go out for an evening. When they finally made it a practice to go anyway, he got the message.

Quite often an evil soul-tie between a mother and child causes a man to forfeit his God-given headship in his adult relationships. Where the umbilical soul-tie to the mother is never completely broken, the son remains in childlike submission to her even after he becomes an adult.

I recall a college classmate whose mother called the college each morning it looked like rain to leave word for her son to be sure to wear his raincoat and boots. This was an unnatural control that she was attempting to continue to maintain over his life. He responded finally by moving to the opposite end of the country to avoid her control. Conversely, if a child, especially a daughter, is unable to bond (form a proper soul-tie) with her father, it can have a lifelong effect upon the young girl. She may spend the rest of her life trying to find the deep bonding and love she has missed. This void may cause her to seek out the very same type of man as her father (alcoholic, drug-addict, one unable to express emotions, womanizer, workaholic), attempting to fill the void within her by completing the bond with the man like her father. Even as an adult, she may still try to find, or complete, the soul-tie which was never fully formed in the formative years of her childhood.

Fortunately, there is One who offers a three-fold solution to being forsaken or unloved by one's parents. He promises that He will fill the void.

> [Jesus] is a **friend** that sticketh closer than a brother.
> Prov. 18:24b

> [Jesus] **will never leave thee**, nor forsake thee.
> Heb. 13:5b

> When my father and my mother forsake me, then the LORD [Jesus] **will take me up**.
> Ps. 27:10

The first night that I began teaching on this subject, a woman happened to attend who told us during the prayer time afterward that she "felt the meeting was just for her." She was under such physical attack that she spent most of the meeting in the restroom. "But," she said, "I heard enough of the teaching to know it was aimed directly at me."

She told us that her mother had plenty of money to be able to enter a nice retirement home, but instead, the mother recently pressured the daughter, against the daughter's will and wishes, to take her into her home. The stress of this episode had made the daughter physically ill.

☞ The mother employed several common, manipulative arguments such as:

- "You are my only child." (obligation)

- "It's your responsibility to take care of me." (duty, obligatory responsibility)

- "Remember all that I have done for you." (more duty, obligation)

- "If you loved me you'd do it." (using love as a weapon of compulsion)

- "What will people think?" (pressure of public opinion)

- "I may not be around much longer." (a manipulative ploy)

- "I might have to cut you out of my will." (financial threat)

This poor daughter was also under the enemy's standard condemnation for not "honoring her mother." Parents often fail, and hurt their children. They may be abusive, alcoholic, cruel, violent, and behave inhumanely toward their children, yet the child still feels tormented and guilty for not loving the parents as Scripture seems to direct. Note that such guilt and condemnation only strengthens unhealthy soul-ties.

UNION WITH FELLOW BELIEVERS

The Scriptures provide a most familiar example of good soul-ties between believers in Jonathan and David:

...the **soul of Jonathan was knit with the soul of David,** and Jonathan loved him as his own soul.

1 Sam. 18:1

Strong's reveals that the word rendered "knit" in this passage is *kaw-shar'* (#7194) as noted earlier in connection with family ties. Jonathan and David actually entered into a covenant relationship. As a result of their covenant, Jonathan attempted to protect David from Saul's rage, and David later cared for Mephibosheth, the last surviving son of Jonathan.

Love is the bond that links souls together in the kingdom of God. It is the very essence of soul-ties in the Body of Christ.

That their hearts might be comforted, **being knit together in love,** and unto all riches of the full assurance of understanding, to the acknowledgment of the mystery of God, and of the Father, and of Christ; In whom are hid all the treasures of wisdom and knowledge.

And not holding the Head, from which all the body by joints and bands having nourishment ministered, and **knit together,** increaseth with the increase of God.

Col. 2:2-3, 19

In these passages, the emphasis is on the believers of God being the family of God.

&❧ The Greek word rendered "being knit together" is *sumbibazo,* pronounced soom-bib-ad-zo (Strong's #822); it means "to drive together, i.e. to unite (in association or affection), compact, gather, instruct, knit together, prove."

The Body of Christ is thus seen to be vitally bound together by means of Godly bonds, or godly soul-ties. God likened the body of believers to a human body, whose members were to be completely linked and interdependent. An Old Testament version of this truth is seen in Judges after the abuse and murder of a concubine.

> So all the men of Israel were gathered against the city, **knit together as one man.**
>
> Judg. 20: 11

The men were united in purpose (in New Testament usage, "in one accord") and became as "one man." Just as there is great power for good in a healthy marital soul-tie, so also is there in a healthy mutual friendship. Two in agreement can form a church!

> For where **two or three** are gathered together in my name, there am I in the midst of them.
>
> Matt. 18:20

The Satanic based counterfeits standing in opposition to the godly ties of friendship are those of so-called lovers or friends who constantly use each other to meet their needs, to build themselves up at the friends' expense, or repeatedly abuse their friendships by betrayals. A friendship soul-tie which experiences betrayal and abuse "spoils" the soul, and certainly ruins the godly benefits of friendship. David experienced this.

> False witnesses did rise up; they laid to my charge things that I knew not. They rewarded me evil for good to the spoiling of my soul. **I behaved myself as though he had been my friend or brother.**
>
> Ps. 35: 11–14a

Thus, a wall, partition, division or block is placed in the relationship. David's soul was "spoiled," damaged by the cruel and unkind actions of others.

David was certainly innocent, but his innocent state did not prevent him from incurring damage to his soul. We observe the same truth in the case of those who were victims of rape, molestation or child abuse by those whom they considered trustworthy. These children too were innocent, yet their souls were damaged, and they often carry great guilt. They need loving ministry to remove the fiery darts and to help heal the wounds. The damage is greatly worsened when the betrayal comes from "the house of a friend."

> Yea, mine own familiar friend, in whom I trusted, which did eat of my bread, hath lifted up his heel against me.
>
> Ps. 41:9

God warns us to not be yoked to unbelievers, or with any of Satan's forces.

> Be ye not **unequally yoked** together with unbelievers: for what **fellowship** hath righteousness with unrighteousness? and what **communion** hath light with darkness?
>
> 2 Cor. 6:14

ə♥ "Unequally yoked" in this passage is *heterozugeó* (Strong's #2086), pronounced het-er-od-zoog-eh-o. It means to yoke up differently, to associate discordantly, to be unequally yoked together.

Many promised to be faithful to God, but proved to be unfaithful. In Scripture we find man being brought into bondage by mere men acting as agents for Satan.

> This matter arose because some false believers had infiltrated our ranks to spy on the freedom we have in Christ Jesus and to **make us slaves**. We did not give in to them for a moment, so that the truth of the gospel might be preserved for you.
>
> Gal. 2:4–5 NIV

These men were merely masquerading as Christian brothers and as leaders. Their goal was not liberty but bondage for the people of God. They attempted to impose their will upon the group to bring it into subjection to their false doctrines. The Scriptural remedy and answer is to resist the lie with the Truth!

All soul-ties and all demonic problems are rooted in untruths or lies spawned by the "father of lies," or by his agents. Such is seen in the above passage referring to "false" or lying brethren. We must especially avoid the demonic stronghold of "believing a lie about God."

Believers should exercise great caution before opening their trusting hearts to another believer who forcefully attempts to impose his or her ways, or the traditions of men. This would include bringing another believer under superstition, public pressure and the opinions of man.

> ...how is it that you are turning back to those weak and miserable forces? Do you wish to be **enslaved by them** all over again? You are observing special days and months and seasons and years!　　Gal. 4:9–10 NIV

> ...[take] up the shield of faith with which you will be able to extinguish all the flaming arrows of the evil one [Satan or his agents].　　Eph. 6:16 NASB [BRACKETS OURS]

MAN AND AUTHORITY FIGURES
(LEADER, PASTOR)

The Scripture establishes a godly relationship of deference and submission to God-established authority.

> ...the men of Judah **clave unto their king**, from Jordan even to Jerusalem.
>
> 2 Sam. 20:2b

> **Submit yourselves** to every ordinance of man for the Lord's sake: whether it be to the king, as supreme; or unto governors... **For so is the will of God...**
>
> 1 Pet. 2:13–15

The church was endowed by Jesus with ministries to build up the faith and maturity of His believers.

> ...When he ascended up on high, he led captivity captive, and gave gifts unto men... And he gave some, apostles; and some, prophets; and some, evangelists; and some, pastors and teachers; For the perfecting of the saints, for the work of the ministry, for the edifying of the body of Christ: Till we all come in the unity of the faith, and of the knowledge of the Son of God, unto a perfect man, unto the measure of the stature of the fulness of Christ...
>
> Eph. 4:8, 11–13

Many people distrust their churches and their government today because of broken soul-ties with their leaders. Men in the churches and government who were trusted, and to whom submission was granted, betrayed that trust and the people were wounded.

Similarly a pastor can only function effectively if the

bonds of love and trust have been established. Trust must be established like that of patient-to-doctor, or of client-to-lawyer. The pastor should have the same spirit of love and concern for the rights and well-being of the believers in his charge that Christ had for His sheep. Love is a two-way street. The same is true of soul-ties; *every soul-tie is a conduit*!

In the Old Testament are several instances of soul-ties between men of God and their leader or authority figure: Joshua and Moses, Elisha and Elijah, and clearly in the New Testament between the disciples and Jesus, and Timothy and Paul.

If man rejects the godly established authority, then the result is rebellion and anarchy. Also by contrast, if the authority is not godly, the results are ungodly: if the head is sick, the body is sick!

Imbalanced soul-ties of devotion that led to self-destruction occurred in WWII, when certain devoted followers of Hitler and Tojo became suicide warriors, such as the Kamikaze pilots of Japan. Their soul-ties and devotion led to the destruction of their very lives and souls.

The Israelites too demonstrated an example of an ungodly bondage to a leader, contrary to the will of God. In this example, the men of Israel rejected David, God's anointed king. The fruit of this was not only to miss God's best, but also to find themselves opposing God.

> So every man of Israel went up from after David, and followed Sheba the son of Bichri...
> 2 Sam. 20:2

THE ACTIONS OF AUTHORITY FIGURES
AFFECT THEIR FOLLOWERS

When King Ahasuerus came under the influence of Haman, there was a spiritual effect upon the people of his kingdom. When the head becomes involved in evil, there is a spirit of confusion loosed that affects those under his headship, and they are not sure what to do or to think. On a conscious level, they may be totally unaware of what is taking place in the mind of their leader, but they are influenced nonetheless.

> And the king and Haman sat down to drink; but **the city Shushan was perplexed** [in confusion].
>
> Esth. 3:15b [BRACKETS OURS]

Correspondingly when the King repented, or when a leader is restored to his right mind, or to Godly behavior, the people will feel a lifting and will rejoice.

> And Mordecai went out from the presence of the king in royal apparel of blue and white, and with a great crown of gold, and with a garment of fine linen and purple: and **the city of Shushan rejoiced and was glad.**
>
> Esth. 8:15–16

When a godly individual was exalted, and the king restored to godliness, the city rejoiced and became glad, no longer perplexed or confused. Notice that the entire city was blessed and rejoiced twofold, with joy and gladness. At the same time the people of God within the same city were perhaps even more blessed, four-fold, receiving light, gladness, joy and honor.

What caused the difference? In the former instance the one in spiritual authority was under the influence of, and cooperating, with evil. In the latter case the king was restored to a godly influence and brought his nation back under God's blessings.

> Obey them that have the rule over you, and submit yourselves: for they **watch for your souls**...
>
> Heb. 13:17

THE MORALS OF A PASTOR LIMIT & AFFECT THE CONGREGATION

I recently spoke with a man who mentioned a relative whom he described as "the greatest person in the world." However, since the time of her divorce, she had been sleeping with the men she was dating. "And the worst part of this" he said, "is that her daughters have been exposed to that example."

I commented, "Yes, and it is highly unlikely that her children will be able to exercise a higher moral standard than that set by their mother."

I was then struck by the thought that the spiritual children of a pastor, i.e. his congregation, will not normally be able to exceed his moral standards, either.

Likewise, when a man in a position of spiritual authority deviates from the truth of Scripture, he opens the door for his flock to be exposed to the same types of error he experiences. If he falls in a particular area of sin, those following him are also vulnerable to that same weakness or sin. This may be due to the soul-ties which can be formed between parishioners and pastor, or to a form of idolatry.

Actions speak louder than words; especially in the case of pastors. The world is little interested in hearing our theology;

they want to see our fruit!

When a pastor breaks his marriage vows, and divorces his wife, expect to see a flurry of divorces in that congregation. Lack of *faith for marriage* spreads through a congregation; then *divorce spirits* spread. The pastor has, at the very least, taught by his actions, that this command of the Lord's is out of date, that it is not as important as has been thought in the past. Thus, the door is opened for the sheep to follow their shepherd into the same form of sin. I recognize that divorce is not the unpardonable sin, but it is frequently an unconfessed sin. This is probably because most women do not want to admit that their choice of husband was a mistake, lest that might somehow require them to return to the former husband whom they may still fear, or hate, or which might put them under judgment. Divorce, which God hates, needs to be confessed like any other sin.

If a pastor harbors erroneous attitudes, false beliefs, corrupted convictions, or distorted doctrines, the errors of these spirits can be transferred to the entire congregation. We are reminded of the warning from Ezekiel concerning the dangers of bonding with false shepherds:

> Thus saith the Lord GOD unto the shepherds; **Woe be to the shepherds of Israel** that do feed themselves! should not the shepherds feed the flocks? ... but ye feed not the flock. The diseased have ye not strengthened, neither have ye healed that which was sick, neither have ye bound up that which was broken, neither have ye brought again that which was driven away, neither have ye sought that which was lost...
>
> Ezek. 34:2–4

In many churches today there is a failure to proclaim the

word of God, and through the word of God, to demonstrate the power of God. This is usually a result of the pastor's cowardice, and of his fear of rejection, fear of failure, fear of loss of prestige, or fear of loss of members.

THE FAITH OF THE PASTOR
LIMITS THE CONGREGATION

I have discovered another surprising truth: the faith of a congregation apparently cannot exceed that of the one in spiritual authority over them. This is why Paul encourages like-minded fellowship. If you are in a church that doesn't believe in healing or deliverance, you will not be able to muster much faith for those benefits, even though you may intellectually believe completely in them. As an example, years ago, we had three men in our fellowship who believed God for the healing of their hernias. Their faith had been ignited in part by the testimony of a skeptic who'd been healed.

Jack, a man to whom I ministered more than twenty five years ago, was scheduled for a double hernia operation. The week before his surgery his friends coerced him into attending a service where I was praying for the sick. He came forward for prayer for his hernias, he related later, "sort of as a joke, not expecting anything to happen." He was very surprised when all his pain left. And when he went the next day for a checkup, the doctor told him, "You no longer have any hernias!"

He was such a skeptic that he went to another doctor and paid for another complete examination which also showed that he no longer had either of the hernias. He came back the next week to the meeting where I was speaking and testified; "I came here last week as a skeptic and I'm still a skeptic, but I have had two different doctors tell me that the two hernias I had prayer for last week no longer exist."

The three men from our weekly fellowship all began attending a local charismatic church on Sundays. The pastor of that church developed a hernia and had a surgical procedure to correct it. Within six months, each of the three men also had hernia surgeries. These men certainly did not sin, but apparently those who place themselves under a spiritual authority do not muster more faith than that possessed by the one to whom they submit themselves.

We have seen more serious types of problems develop among others whom we have referred to a certain local church, which formerly was charismatic in its orientation, but has since changed pastors and become virtually anti-charismatic in its theology. That church has since experienced an epidemic of various types of cancer, after losing a pastor to cancer. Subsequently, after a succeeding pastor committed suicide, numerous church members have been plagued by depression and suicidal thoughts.

MAN AND HIS FELLOW CITIZENS

Positive bonds can develop between citizens of a particular region when they unite against some form of threat to the community. The citizens of the Allied countries during WWII made great sacrifices and joined together to help achieve victory over Fascism. Community organizations unite souls to combat a wide variety of evils: drugs, crime, and other forms of injustice. These bonds can lead to lasting friendships formed on common definitions of public good.

Sometimes this goes terribly wrong, however, when people

unite to break God's societal laws, as gangs, vigilantes, or mobs. There is tremendous potential power in the uniting of souls, either to bring life or death to a community.

Cultic Soul-Ties

Soul-ties normally exist within cultic organizations. A linking of the people occurs through mind-control usually in mutual allegiance to a cultic leader or to cultic beliefs and doctrines, such as white supremacy, or satanic beliefs.

Unfortunately, as we have previously demonstrated, some soul-ties are ungodly, unnatural and evil. A negative soul-tie is subtle, and like a cancer, grows slowly, undetected. If you never look in a mirror, you won't discover the smudge of dirt on your face. The perfect law of liberty is the Word of God, the mirror to discover flaws that need correcting.

Satan, through a spirit of anti-Christ, has always fervently sought to draw man's soul after himself, and he uses self-centered individuals, cults and gurus, and the occult. Man can literally sell his soul through a conscious pledge of allegiance to a satanic religion or its representatives. The fact that man may not fully believe in Satan's reality and power does not prevent him from bonding his soul to the devil, through ungodly spiritual activity. There is no gray area of non-commitment. Man was created to be in relationship with the invisible, the spiritual, and has to make a conscious decision to unite his soul to Christ. That is the ultimate good soul-tie and by any standard the greatest one of all.

Witchcraft

An evil soul-tie is actually a form of witchcraft. Witchcraft is spiritual. It is essentially defined as one person's control over another person.

☞ *Witchcraft* - the manipulation, control, or domination of one person by another person. Unhealthy soul ties between individuals are often a form of *witchcraft*, to varying degrees.

For example, if I were exercising witchcraft on you, I would be attempting to get you to do my will by a power that is not the Holy Spirit. The power involved is, in the best light, a form of psychic or soulish power, and is at worst satanic or demonic. Satan is the author of bondages and loves to see people restricted, tormented, helpless or hopeless. This is the subtle form of witchcraft or control practiced by one person over another.

CONSCIOUS WITCHCRAFT

Overt witchcraft involves conscious awareness of what is being done. The source of the power is not of God but comes through an occult practitioner. The one practicing it is either himself a witch/warlock, or has employed the assistance of an actual practitioner of witchcraft to place the spell, or curse, upon the other party. There is no such thing as "white witchcraft," there is only witchcraft.

In conjuring up such spells the practitioner may use personal items, such as hair or articles of clothing to work the spell. The spells have various effects: the individual may be unable to sleep, find himself tormented, unable to have financial success (losing jobs, etc.), unable to make friends, estranged from old friends, or unable to find any peace unless he returns to the person he or she has left. Such spells may have such wording as: "Bring Joe back to me; don't ever let him be happy with anyone else! Don't let him have any satisfaction until he returns. Make him come back! Give him trouble until he marries me!"

One of the most common characteristics of witchcraft is its emasculation of males. Witchcraft is traditionally matriarchal. The women wear the pants; the role of the man is either abdicated or usurped, resulting in his emasculation.

UNCONSCIOUS WITCHCRAFT

The person who simply "prays amiss" may be making the very same pronouncements, but is unaware that he or she is practicing unconscious witchcraft, and unaware that the power of Satan is being utilized. The person may not even believe in Satan or in witchcraft. However, the power is still the same.

A prayer uttered because of a need for revenge or control can create a source of harassment against the other person. If a soul-tie has existed between the two, this unconscious form of control or witchcraft practiced by one will continue to oppress the other.

Every prayer is heard, but the question is by whom? God does not honor prayers of revenge or manipulation — but we firmly believe Satan does. A believer praying in the wrong spirit can harm the other with subtle oppression. It is extremely important that we guard our prayers by praying according to the will of God. God has made it abundantly clear that we are allowed to pour out our complaints before Him, but we must divest ourselves of unforgiveness, resentment, and bitterness. A good way to pray concerning one who has offended you is:

Lord Jesus, I forgive their actions. Please draw them closer to You. If they refuse to respond to Your Spirit, then I release them to experience the consequences of their own delusions, in hope that they might again *Yes!!!* turn to you."

Amen.

If Jesus forgave those who disregarded Him, then we should as well.

> The disciple is not above his master, nor the servant above his lord.
>
> Matt. 10:24

The concept of unconscious witchcraft, i.e. subtle control, is brought out forcefully in Jesus' lament in Matthew 11:

> But whereunto shall I liken this generation? It is like unto children sitting in the markets, and calling unto their fellows, And saying, We have piped unto you, and ye have not danced; we have mourned unto you, and ye have not lamented. For John came neither eating nor drinking, and they say, He hath a devil. The Son of man came eating and drinking, and they say, Behold a man gluttonous, and a winebibber, a friend of publicans and sinners. But wisdom is justified of her children.
>
> Matt. 11:16–19

The consideration here in Matthew 11 is not whether one fasted or ate, mourned or danced, but whether one followed the command of the leaders, those in control. Control was the real issue.

We tend to be the most vulnerable to those closest to us. We are rarely subject even to the subtle domination of a stranger. The key to avoiding such bondages is to know the truth about soul-ties and thus to be forewarned, and forearmed, to be able to willfully resist them.

Witchcraft can operate in one of two ways: through aggression (forcefully demanding submission to one's will), and through weakness and need (submission through guilt). Either way, ungodly "strings" can become attached to one's soul.

Controlling people are very selfish and want their needs met. This is the opposite of the Christian who is *to serve, like Jesus*, who came not to be served, but to serve.

> Ye know that they that... rule over the Gentiles exercise lordship over them... But so **shall it not be among you:** but whosoever will be great among you... shall be servant of all.
>
> Mark 10:42–44

The one attempting to control you or others around him usually is motivated himself by some type of fear, often a fear of rejection. This fear frequently is rooted in abandonment experienced during childhood. Thus the goal of the one who is abusing you is to exercise control over his circumstances so that no one can hurt or reject him again.

The need for love and acceptance is far too great for anyone to fill. Because it is often a void or need rooted in abandonment from childhood,[1] it can only be filled by the love of an earthly father or resolved by the supernatural ministry of the Spirit through lovingly administered deliverance.

Although the controlling person may be a professing Christian, he or she has not fully yielded to the Holy Spirit. The Holy Spirit doesn't coerce; He gently and lovingly leads, following the pattern set by the Good Shepherd.

Parents may attempt to manipulate married children into spending the holidays with them. The daughter for example may have to tell her mother that she has to go to her husband's family for Christmas. The reaction may be quite emotional with tears and exclamations such as, "You don't love us anymore!" Another response may be anger, which catches newlyweds by surprise. It may even include name calling or threats, implied or actually stated.

> Death and life are in the power of the tongue...
> Prov. 18:21a

Words can hurt, even when we are adults. Veiled or non-veiled threats can hurt. "If you don't come here for Christmas, don't bother coming back later." "If you don't come here for Thanksgiving, you'll no longer be my son [or my daughter]." "Don't expect me to help with your college bills any longer." "If you don't honor your family, you'll never succeed."

Another devious ploy is "giving the silent treatment;" to stop talking to the offending person, to cut off all communication. This is ungodly, and hurtful. A single strand of string won't prevent you from pulling away, but if you allow someone to tie

---

[1] Usually as the result of an absent father or parent. See *Deliverance for Children and Teens*, by same author. Available at www.impactchristianbooks.com

you with twelve strands of string, you are just as bound as if you had been bound with a twelve-stranded rope.

When you realize that there are "strings" attached to something that someone offers to you, or offers to do for you, this should cause an immediate check. The key to maintaining freedom is to resist the first string as soon as you discern it, even if it is only slightly restrictive of your freedom. There is an applicable principle in the Scriptures concerning spiritual warfare which I love to quote:

> The roaring of the lion, and the voice of the fierce lion,
> and the teeth of the young lions, **are broken**.
>
> Job 4:10

Many of us would feel inadequate to go up against a full-grown lion in his strength, but feel we could handle a young lion cub. We can kill the young lions, or **pull their teeth**. We can remove today the fangs that might later kill us, by dealing with them in advance.

The useful principle here is this: *fight the battle while your enemies are still small*; do not let your enemies grow up. Do not let them become strongly entrenched.

This is especially true in regard to ungodly soul-ties. If you begin to feel that there is something unhealthy about a relationship, nip it in the bud! Withdraw yourself, pull back to safety, and regroup. While involved in a controlling relationship, it is very difficult to even get a good perspective upon your own situation!

CHRISTIAN WITCHCRAFT & CHRISTIAN SOUL-TIES

This may require explanation as the terms seem to be contradictory. Unfortunately, it is a reality. There is a form of witchcraft that exists within churches. Many churches have one family or one person who runs the show, who is the power behind the throne. He may be the individual who is most wealthy, or the largest contributor, who says, "I'll buy the church a new organ, *but* we must have a new choir director, *first*!" "I'll buy the new carpet, *but* it must be blue!"

These demands may seem relatively insignificant, but that individual has usurped the prerogative of either the pastor, or the church's board, to vote upon such expenditures. These are obvious examples of control. More frequently, the control is subtle, being exercised merely as an opinion, "I don't think Brother Jones is capable of handling the duties of a deacon." However, that opinion carries the weight of the one who is the major financial supporter of the church, and carries an implied threat of "Take my opinion seriously, or run the risk of losing my support."

Once such control begins, and is allowed to exist by either the church or the pastor, God is no longer in control of that church. Rather, the power-wielding individual is in control. Thus, the pastor and fellow members come into soul-bondage to the wealthy member.

Other soul bondages can develop within a church or group when one member seems more spiritual than others. If not carefully discerned, one's prophetic "gift" may become a powerful source of manipulation and control.

Recently we have seen some in a Christian context abuse

and control those under them, such as Jim Jones at Jonestown, David Koresch outside Waco, and the tragedy involving the Heaven's Gate suicides. In these instances, the pastors involved apparently operated with a counterfeit anointing, or a demonic anointing, with which they held people under their spell.

Jim Jones started out with a mighty anointing of God upon his life. A fellow pastor told me that in the early days of his ministry, Jones had conducted a healing service in his church. At one point he walked up to a woman who had a large, purple cancerous growth upon her cheek and placed his handkerchief over the growth and it came off in the handkerchief. Unfortunately, the ability to work miracles does not preclude an individual from misusing his or her gift to control the lives of others. Such subtle witchcraft is surely "lawlessness" in God's eyes.

> Not every one that saith unto me, Lord, Lord, shall enter into the kingdom of heaven; but he that doeth the will of my Father which is in heaven. Many will say to me in that day, Lord, Lord, have we not prophesied in thy name? and in thy name have cast out devils? and in thy name done many wonderful works? And then will I profess unto them, I never knew you: depart from me, ye that work iniquity.
>
> Matt. 7:21–23

CONTROL ATTEMPTED THROUGH PROPHECY

Another case of attempted control, which I encountered personally, came in connection with a prophecy. At the close of a large charismatic meeting in the early seventies, a man I did not know came to me and announced with great excitement, "My wife received a prophecy during tonight's meeting. The

Lord told her that 'If you and I go into the book business together, He would bless us with tremendous success!' What do you think of that?" He asked, breathless with excitement.

I should point out that at the time I was already in the book business, he was not.

I responded bluntly, "Brother, I don't witness to it, for three reasons. My first check is: if it was a valid prophecy, then why didn't your wife give it publicly and let the Body judge it, as the Scripture instructs, (*Let the prophets speak two or three and let the other judge.* [1 Cor. 14:29]). Secondly, since I am already in the business, it would have been more logical for the Lord to give me the message about taking you on as a partner. Third, I have absolutely no agreement in my spirit with the prophecy. I believe that if God had indeed spoken that message to your wife, then He would have prepared agreement, or receptivity, in my heart to receive His message. Since there is none, I must assume that it was not from Him."

Needless to say, the young man did not agree with my assessment and stomped off in a huff.

I do not believe this was necessarily a demonically-inspired message. There are three possible sources of prophecy: the Holy Spirit, an evil spirit, or a misguided human spirit. This was, I suspect, simply the fruit of the woman's own desire to be involved in a Christian business and ministry. It came from *her head*, rather than from the Holy Spirit, for at least the reasons outlined above.

Prophecy can easily be misused to place someone in bondage to "a prophet." A true prophet of God will strive to prevent people from becoming dependent upon him! (see Acts 14:14).

Many Christians are so hungry for a true word from God that they will follow willingly after prophets, due to their desire to hear a private word. There are some ministries which are built upon the practice of giving personal words of prophecy.

Although it is certainly true that God does, upon occasion, speak words of direction to individuals, much of this seeking is misdirected. In some cases, it reflects laziness or an unwillingness to put forth enough effort to seek God personally. Such seeking can also have a selfish motivation, which added to the expectation of receiving personal direction, makes the hearer extremely vulnerable to abuses of prophecy, control, and a soul-tie to the "prophet."

Another form of self-elevation which leads to soul-ties of control and dependency is often found among leaders of cults, and even some churches (large or small). The source of control is having the latest, unique "revelation." God certainly grants revelations in his Word, to His people, to His servants, and to His teachers. However, those revelations are also confirmable, or verifiable, to any believer by simply checking the Scriptures.

> ...no prophecy of the scripture is of any private interpretation.
>
> 2 Pet. 1:20

It is the anxious individual who constantly feels the need to know the future who most often forms unhealthy soul-ties with fortune-tellers and prophets.

As we have seen, God intended man to experience a oneness not only with Himself, but also with his fellow man. In this we may enjoy His blessings and the world may recognize His working.

> That they all may be one; as thou, Father, art in me, and I in thee, that they also may be one in us: that the world may believe that thou hast sent me.
>
> John 17:21

However, as is the case with all of God's plans, Satan brings his own perversions and counterfeits to bear, in an attempt not only to damage our souls, but also to harm others with a ripple effect.

In the following chapter, we will see how these counterfeits may enter our lives.

First, consider the contrasts between the righteous and unrighteous effects of good and evil soul-ties indicated in the chart on the two following pages.

The following chart summarizes at a glance the resulting effects of both healthy and unhealthy soul types.

GODLY SOUL-TIES

MARRIAGE

1. The Bonds of **Marriage** cause husband and wife to become *one flesh*, and properly submit to each other in a lifetime commitment.

FAMILY

2. The **Bonds of Family** are normally characterized by loving relationships, open communication and forgiveness, with properly loved and disciplined children.

FRIENDSHIP

3. The Bonds of **Friendship** are characterized by mutual love, respect and trust.

DESTRUCTIVE SOUL-TIES

MARRIAGE

1. **Adultery** causes an unfaithful partner to fuse his or her soul to another.

   Unhealthy control of one partner over the other through either aggressive dominance or demanding weakness. May be evidenced by separation and divorce.

FAMILY

2. **Alienation** of affections through too much control exercised by a parent or a child; evidenced by a crippling of the child's future adult relationships.

FRIENDSHIP

3. **Abuse** by another due to jealousy or constant demanding needs, or an uncontrollable need to be in charge of another's life. Seen in hurt feelings and wounded souls.

AUTHORITY

4. **The Bonds of Proper Submission** are formed with someone placed in Godly authority, as a leader, king, elder, pastor, boss.

4. **Complete obedience** to leaders who either manifest ungodly wisdom, or demand ungodly allegiance, causing the submissive one to break loyalty to God. Evidenced by loss of spiritual freedom and failure in personal life.

BODY FELLOWSHIP

5. **Bonds of Love for Fellow Believers** are characterized by loving one another, servanthood, kindness, tolerance and honesty.

5. **Inability to unify** or, in a greater sense, to accomplish the Great Commission, because of schisms, denominationalism, leader-idolatry, and tolerating "sin in the camp." Evidenced by self-righteous pride.

FELLOWSHIP WITH GOD

6. **Bonds of Love and Service to God** are characterized by love, joy, peace, righteousness and the freedom which allows God-dependency over man-dependency, permitting both the gifts and the fruit of the Spirit to operate freely.

6. **Inability to relate to a personal God** due to the influence of satanic practices, cults and the occult. Evidenced by confusion, inability to concentrate on or to remember Scripture, and an inability to manifest self-control.

3

THE DEVELOPMENT OF HARMFUL ADULT SOUL-TIES THROUGH CHOICES WE MAKE

How Do Negative Soul-Ties Develop?

How are bondages such as soul-ties formed? Consider how people became bondservants in the early history of our country. They were given a choice of coming here as bond-servants to work off their indebtedness. Thus they were sold into bondage as slaves, or were simply poor people who sold themselves into bondservanthood to earn the price of a passage to the new world.[2] This is an example of bondage in the natural world, and corresponds to the types of bondage we see in the supernatural realm.

Some were criminals who had been imprisoned for acts committed against society and were granted the option of

---

[2] These are certainly not the only roots of demonic activity; for example, someone can *inherit* a spirit of alcoholism.

coming to America as bondservants to work off a sentence. Some were men who were poor, or heavily in debt, often from debtors' prisons, who sold themselves or their families into voluntary servitude to escape England and debts they could not pay. Recall the words of the song, "We owed a debt we could not pay: He came and paid a debt He did not owe!"

Of course when bondage or slavery is mentioned, we think immediately of slaves brought from Africa to work in the Southern States. But bondservants were usually indentured to their masters as a result of their own decisions.

Jesus came to set the captives free. Who were the captives? Who were the slaves? We are the captives; we are the slaves who have willingly or unwittingly sold ourselves into bondage to the enemy through rebellion, pride, lust, etc.

Bondage develops in situations that are as overt as slavery and indentured servitude, or through more subtle agreements between two parties or even with one's self. Secretive associations or ties to secret societies also lead to harmful soul-ties. Lack of knowledge allows many unhealthy ties to develop.

> Therefore my people are gone into captivity, because **they have no knowledge**: and their honourable men are famished, and their multitude dried up with thirst.
>
> Isa. 5:13

> My people are **destroyed for lack of knowledge**:
>
> Hosea 4:6a

Jesus has provided His followers with both *exousia* (legal authority) and *dunamis* (enabling power) to do His will.

However, authority and power must both be taken up, and utilized, or are of no effect, just as the blood of the Passover Lamb had to be applied to the door posts or it offered no protection against the Angel of Death.

Jesus illustrated His will for the souls of His people to be freed, through his actions. He set souls free, and restored both minds and souls via deliverance, and commends us to do the same.

> And Jesus went about all Galilee, teaching in their synagogues, and preaching the gospel of the kingdom, and healing all manner of sickness and all manner of disease among the people, And his fame went throughout all Syria: and they brought unto him all sick people that were taken with divers diseases and torments, **and those which were possessed with devils,** and those which were lunatic, and those that had the palsy; and **he healed them.**
>
> Matt. 4:23-24

AGREEMENT BETWEEN TWO PARTIES

Agreement is at the core of every relationship created between human beings; the power of agreement lies in human choice.

> Can two walk together, except they be agreed?
>
> Amos 3:3

The oldest and strongest bond possible between two parties is that of a blood covenant, an integral part of which is the basic agreement between the parties as to the terms of their agreement. Covenants are the basis of relationship within supernatural kingdoms also. Satan attempts to copy

God's methods whenever possible, and his followers, such as his witches, are in covenant with him. Thus the origin of the witchcraft term, "coven."

The New Testament teaches to shun evil, and avoid those who are its carriers.

> Be ye not unequally yoked together with unbelievers: for what fellowship hath righteousness with unrighteousness? and what communion hath light with darkness?
>
> 2 Cor. 6:14

If we allow ourselves to bond with those we know are engaging in sin, we become a partaker of their sin, and the evil spirits within them can easily pass to us. Even though we may enter such a relationship hoping to help that other person, to lift them up by our witness, usually the exact opposite occurs. The pull of their sin wears us down and we weaken, discovering that our own standards have been lowered. We are instructed in Scripture to avoid associating with evil companions or those from whom we might learn sin or bad habits. In the Old Testament, God often eliminated entire communities of people who were tainted by, or contaminated with, sin lest other souls might become snared.

> Make no friendship with an angry man; and with a furious man thou shalt not go: Lest thou learn his ways, and get a snare to thy soul.
>
> Prov. 22:24-25

> Be sober, be vigilant; because your adversary the devil, as a roaring lion, walketh about, seeking whom he may devour.
>
> 1 Pet. 5:8

SECRECY BUILDS SOUL-TIES

The Devil, like the spider, seeks to trap his victims in a snare of sin so that he might the more easily devour them. One of the most insidious ways of creating bondage is to establish a bond of secrecy. "Don't tell anyone what I'm going to tell you." You and that person are thus bound in an unholy bond of gossip and darkness, and you share in the guilt, which is why Jesus warns in the Scripture:

> But let your communication be, Yea, yea; Nay, nay: for whatsoever is more than these cometh of evil.
>
> Matt. 5:37

And,

> Therefore whatsoever ye have spoken in darkness shall be heard in the light...
>
> Luke 12:3

The prescription in the fifth chapter of James requires open confession before trusted elders. If you ask me not to reveal that you have killed someone, and I continue to keep your secret, I am allying myself with you, not only legally as an accomplice, but I am also spiritually sharing your guilt.

> And **have no fellowship with the unfruitful** works of **darkness,** but rather reprove them. For it is a shame even to speak of those things which are done of them in secret.
>
> Eph. 5:11–12

Others commit sins that require a partner or a collaborator, and thus involve the maintenance of secrecy. This creates the additional fear of exposure. Drugs often entrap both the user and those who enable them in secrecy. So too with abuse, where the victim is often unable to get the help they need, or is afraid to try.

SOUL-TIES FORM IN CLOSED OR SECRET ORGANIZATIONS

Anything secret is a work perpetuated in darkness and should be renounced. A classic example would be membership in any type of a secret society, no matter how innocuous or innocent such involvement may seem. One needs to consider breaking ties with such organizations as the Boy Scouts which have secret oaths and forms of Indian witchcraft in the upper levels. Similar organizations are Indian Guides, all college fraternities or sororities with secret initiatory rites, and all such organizations as Masonry, DeMolay, PEO, Eastern Star, Rosicrucian Order, Knights of Columbus, or any other fraternal or secret societies, regardless of the respect such organizations might enjoy in a particular community.

A test for an inappropriate soul-tie to an organization and/ or its members is whether you are required to keep a secret oath, and are unwilling, or unable, to reveal the terms of the oath to a brother or sister in Christ, or even to a minister.

The refusal to uncover the secret and expose it to the light of day, and to break with it, is a tacit decision to remain in bondage to the organization or person whose secrecy is being maintained.

Soul-Ties can also be Formed with Open Organizations

One must also break soul-ties with churches, companies or any organizations which keep one from going on with God. One is often encouraged to "put your heart and soul into an activity." Be wary of sentimental ties to anything. In reality, soul-ties form between the people within these organizations, and their demands upon your time often infringe upon your commitment to God.

Legalism and tradition can quickly quench the Spirit. Even though we may feel that our presence in an organization will have a positive effect for Jesus, we must be free to withdraw if we sense spiritual dryness or heaviness settling upon our hearts. Just as the Tabernacle in the wilderness was portable and was moved when and where the Presence went, so must a believer remain sufficiently independent from others in a church to participate in other fellowships, if God leads him to do so.

Agreement Through Sexual Bondages

"I lost my heart to her!" "I gave her my heart!" "My life is wrapped up in her/him!" "She/he stole my heart!" "She/he is my life." These poor confessions build unhealthy soul-ties with an ex-wife, husband, fiancée, or with a sexual partner or lover, especially when consummated with adultery, fornication, or homosexual activities.

The hardest ties for the victim to understand, and for the one ministering to discover, are those ties formed through relationships which seemed innocent, where "nothing happened" (i.e. there was neither physical contact nor any sexual contact). Yet, somehow, soul-ties were formed and the bondages exist, based on the testimonies of the people involved. The symptoms may be identical to those where there was actual sexual contact. This may be explained in part by Jesus' statement:

> But I say unto you, That whosoever **looketh** on a woman to lust after her hath committed adultery with her already in his heart.
>
> Matt. 5:28

Merely looking with wrong motivation can be very dangerous, as King David learned, much to his regret.

PORNOGRAPHIC SOUL-TIES

Pornography can create a soul-tie with the object of lust. For example, a man who never met a Hollywood star can have a soul-tie with her image. Through such images, and acts of masturbation, he has idolized her, or has had her as a sexual partner in his fantasy. There is a very real tie that can form — a giving up of a part of one's self to the object of lust.

God takes a harsh view toward sexual sins:

> But the fearful, and unbelieving, and the abominable, and murderers, and **whoremongers**, and sorcerers, and idolaters, and all liars, shall have their part in the lake which burneth with fire and brimstone.
>
> Rev. 21:8

Sexual soul-ties are often created by a man looking upon a woman's body, beholding her nakedness. Sin enters via the eye gate, by looking upon her... and lust results. The same thing can happen to women who look at the nakedness of a man, or allow their thoughts to linger unchecked upon him. A confirmation of the concept of looking in lust leading to a soul-tie is found in Scripture.

> And when Shechem the son of Hamor the Hivite, prince of the country, saw her, he took her, and lay with her, and defiled her. And his **soul clave** unto Dinah the daughter of Jacob, and he loved the damsel...
>
> Gen. 34:2–3

The same thing happens when we choose adulterous relationships, or open ourselves up to demonic ties through Internet pornography.

> Know ye not that your bodies are the members of Christ? **shall I then take the members of Christ, and make them the members of an harlot?** God forbid. What? know ye not that he which is joined to an harlot is one body? for two, saith he, shall be one flesh.
>
> 1 Cor. 6:15–16

FORNICATION AND ADULTERY

A common unhealthy and evil soul-tie exists between ex-lovers who have not married each other. By definition these individuals have entered into a sexual union by which they have been made "one flesh" outside the covenants of God. They have entered into a union and consummated that union sexually, becoming thereby one flesh. The result is a lingering soul-tie. The problem of being "love-sick" or "heart-sick" is a reality. Even Shakespeare wrote of such cases.

Some experience obsession because of these ties, and this

can become extremely tormenting. It is not uncommon to encounter those who testify that their minds are tortured, and that they are unable to get the words, or images, of the other partner out of their thoughts. Psychology speaks of this condition as a mind-link; we see it as a soul-tie.

This phenomenon usually manifests when the relationship is threatened, when one of the lovers is attempting to break off contact with the other. This is not the compulsion simply to see one another, often experienced by those in love when a relationship is breaking up or doing badly, but rather a compulsion bordering upon an obsession to be with that person, even though mentally, the person wills to be free from the other party.

There is a union that occurs when two individuals are sexually united;, as their bodies merge, so also, to some degree, do their souls merge. The result is a union, albeit temporary. However, the fruit of that union can be relatively permanent. For instance, if human conception occurs, a child will be the result: a visible, tangible, lifetime, memorial expression of the union that occurred. There is also an invisible memorial, an expression of that union in the form of a sexual soul-tie, which will likewise last a lifetime, or until it is recognized, its hold broken, and its residue expelled.

A child is a memorial of the relationship that exists between the parents. The soul-tie is a memorial of the sin (lust) that existed between the unmarried couple. Both the child and the soul-tie serve as reminders to the couples of their relationship.

The righteous soul-ties that God designed and intended for marriage can be corrupted into unrighteous soul-ties, as can happen when marriages break up and divorce results. As in most soul-ties formed from illicit sexual union, the love expressed usually turns to abject and dangerous hate when the tie is broken. Such is found also in the story of King David's daughter Tamar, which provides another Scriptural example of a soul-tie formed in fornication and immorality.

> And when she had brought them unto him to eat, he took hold of her, and said unto her, Come lie with me, my sister. And she answered him, Nay, my brother, do not force me; for no such thing ought to be done in Israel: do not thou this folly. And I, whither shall I cause my shame to go? and as for thee, thou shalt be as one of the fools in Israel. Now therefore, I pray thee, speak unto the king; for he will not withhold me from thee. Howbeit he would not hearken unto her voice: but, being stronger than she, forced her, and lay with her. Then Amnon hated her exceedingly; so that **the hatred wherewith he hated her was greater than the love wherewith he had loved her.** And Amnon said unto her, Arise, be gone. And she said unto him, There is no cause: this evil in sending me away is greater than the other that thou didst unto me. But he would not hearken unto her.
>
> 2 Sam. 13:11–16

Tamar points out to Amnon that the evil of sending her away, rejecting her, was worse than his original sin of forcing her into sexual union. The commentary of the Word of God itself is enlightening in this case. It points out that the resulting hatred of Amnon was greater than the initial love which caused him to sin in the first place, a clear example of love turned into hate. This condition is not uncommon in our day, and is often observed both in divorces, and the breakup of non-marital relationships. The fact that hate exists in these cases is indicative that the soul-tie has not been broken, even if the relationship has. Hate forms its own chain, linking two people.

Witchcraft invariably uses sex to attack and bring down men (and women) of God. I wish it were not the case, but we can all think of cases of nationally known ministers who were caught in sexual snares and scandals which have brought reproach upon the Body of Christ. In my prayer room during deliverance, I have had witches admit to using sex and drugs to lure men under their control. I pray the following condemnation may never be spoken of us.

> For the name of God is blasphemed among the Gentiles through you, [lit: "as a result of your actions"]
>
> Rom. 2:24 [BRACKETS OURS]

It is also obvious that *evil spirits* seek an opportunity to ensnare vulnerable souls who become entrapped in situations involving fallen men and women, as Proverbs 7 warns:

> And behold, a woman comes to meet him, Dressed as a harlot and cunning of heart. With her many persuasions she entices him... Suddenly he follows her... As a bird hastens to the snare, So he does not know that it will cost him his life.
>
> Prov. 7:10,21-23 NASB

Many years ago, a woman from our own prayer group confessed to my wife after a prayer meeting that she had wanted to seduce me.

"But it really isn't Bill I wanted to seduce; it's the Christian bookstore, the publishing company and the entire supernatural ministry of healing and deliverance." Her aim was to control the move of the Holy Spirit through the seduction of a leader.

Yet, because of her honesty and repentance, she was delivered and is still walking with the Lord today, more than twenty years later.

> The Lord's bond-servant must not be quarrelsome, but be kind to all, able to teach, patient when wronged, with gentleness correcting those who are in opposition, if perhaps God may grant them repentance leading to the knowledge of the truth, and they may come to their senses and escape from **the snare of the devil**, having been held captive by him **to do his will**
>
> 2 Tim. 2:24–26 NASB

SEXUAL PERVERSIONS

Homosexuality, lesbianism, and other forms of perversion cause ungodly links of guilt, shame, and sin. Extremely strong soul-ties are often formed between individuals involved in such relationships.

> Thou shalt not lie with mankind, as with womankind: it is abomination.
>
> Lev. 18:22

Quite often, we have found that it is a young child or teen who is led into a homosexual lifestyle by an older man or woman. Once the child is taken advantage of or abused sexually, the door is opened through illicit sexual encounter for unhealthy soul-ties to form with the same sex. Sin and guilt combine to create a barrier of hidden shame.

AGREEMENT BY TWO PARTIES
TO ACCOMPLISH EVIL CONSPIRACIES

Herod and Pilate became allied against Jesus:

> And the same day Pilate and Herod were made friends together: for before they were at enmity between themselves.
>
> Luke 23:12

They were united by agreement in rebellion against God. They became bound together in a friendship of sorts. We have expressions that describe this type of activity: "Birds of a feather flock together" or "They are thicker than thieves" are two examples.

The Scriptures contain many examples of the enemies of God banding together against His anointed ones. Consider the enemies of Joseph, the enemies of David, and the enemies of Jesus Christ, all of whom united to oppose them in agreement against the will and working of God. This united opposition is to be seen in several Scriptures.

> ...for the Jews **had agreed already**, that if any man did confess that he was Christ, he should be put out of the synagogue.
>
> John 9:22

> ...How is it that ye have **agreed together** to tempt the Spirit of the Lord?
>
> Acts 5:9a

> Now the chief priests, and elders, and all the council, **sought false witness** against Jesus, to put him to death;
>
> Matt. 26:59

Then gathered the chief priests and the Pharisees a council... Then from that day forth they **took counsel together for to put him to death.**

John 11:47–53

When a person seeks to harm another, he often requires an accomplice. Gossip unites or binds people together in a common assault against someone else. Be careful not to enter into harmful gossip; you may find yourself bound to the soul of one who unrighteously seeks to harm another.

AGREEMENT THROUGH AN OBLIGATION

Man often comes into a soul-tie of agreement because of bondages of obligation, sometimes introduced through a sense of false responsibility, and other times introduced through gifts or assistance that are given with an expected obligation.

☞ Watch out for "the strings" when you hear statements like:

- "You had better do this for me now, remember I won't be around much longer."

- "You know your brother (or sister) would do this for me."

- "If you don't do this for me, I don't know if my heart can stand the strain."

☞ Soul-ties of false responsibility are a form of bondage, and are based on a lie. These lines may feed our egos but are simply not true.

- "Only you can save me."

- "You are the only person who can help me with my problem."

- "No one else can witness to me like you can."

Obligation can be created by some kind of preferential treatment. For example, the firstborn grandson or granddaughter is selected as a favorite and treated differently than the other grandchildren. It is not uncommon for this to cause jealousy and rejection by siblings, as was the case with Joseph and the special gift of a coat. The effect of such rejection results in even more dependence upon the one favoring the child.

The adult gets their hooks, chains, or cords of bondage established in that individual by granting a favored status and by "loving them more," but it is conditional love and therefore the specter of losing that status remains constantly in the background. The child is in an unstable relationship, and fear is present because the favored status is somehow, in a vague, ill-defined way, conditional upon continually pleasing the donor. Or, the conditional love requires continually proving oneself to meet the unstated standard.

GIFTS

How can one differentiate between good and bad gifts? The key resides primarily in the motivation of the sender. What does he or she hope to gain by giving the gift? Is the motivation godly or ungodly? What is expected in return? Are there strings attached to the gift?

☞ A *test for bad gifts* would include the following questions:

- Do you have a bad feeling about the gift?

- Has the Spirit given you a check in your spirit?

- Is the gift inappropriate?

- Did it cost too much?

Is it too personal? For example, a man giving lingerie to a married woman is inappropriate. Gifts often create an unhealthy obligation. Jewelry is often such a gift. Rings particularly are used to bind someone, and often excused or disguised as rings of "friendship." They are usually inappropriate.

Years ago the husband of a professional tennis player came for ministry, seeking help to recover his wife from a lesbian society connected to women tennis players. This perverted group sent the young wife to a "special trainer," someone who also indoctrinated women sexually. At the close of the training sessions, she gave each woman a ring. Afterward, there were strong soul-ties bound to that perverted society.

Most of us are not used to thinking in such terms, nor are we in the habit of looking a gift horse in the mouth, but we need to be wary of any gift that we feel is in some way inappropriate. Any gift received which the recipient would be unwilling to publicly acknowledge having received, is probably an inappropriate gift.

We were called for help in a case that involved a female

prayer group leader who complained of confusion and mind-blockages. She also mentioned having been repeatedly sent expensive gifts by a woman in her prayer group. She, and we, finally determined there were lesbian overtones to the gifts. When they were all returned or destroyed, the woman's power over the prayer group leader was broken.

Gifts of large sums of money given by one family member to another can create a great bondage of obligation and soul control.

ASSISTANCE

Even assistance can create bondage if strings are attached. The bondages may not come directly as the result of a gift, but rather as the result of "help extended," often in a time of need. For example, someone pays your fine or bails you out of jail, and thus puts you under obligation.

How may we determine whether a gift or action is intended to create a problem for us? Is there a test? The difference between a kind act and a manipulative act tends to be determined by ascertaining whether there are "strings" attached to the act, and whether you feel free to subsequently "walk away."

A parent or friend may perform valid acts of generosity, or again, there may be strings attached.

☞ If there are manipulative phrases such as the following attached, beware:

- "I'll buy this for you, if..."

- "Your father and I will buy you a house, if you'll live next door to us."

- ◆ "If you really loved me, you would..."

- ◆ "Don't tell your father, and I'll buy it for you."

- ◆ "This is a family heirloom, and I have always wanted you to have it. However, if you don't use it [i.e. put it on display], I want it back."

- ◆ "We'll pay for the remodeling of your home, but don't let your husband take that job out of town."

Notice that all of the above are *conditional*, and have the effect of exercising control, manipulation, or domination over the one on the receiving end. This is actually witchcraft, and puts one in bondage to the will, wishes, demands or control of the other party.

Through yielding to such pressures, and failing to resist this type of control, one can become vulnerable to a soul-tie. In fact, each time one gives in to such control, *the soul-tie grows stronger*, and becomes increasingly harder to break.

Moses gives us an excellent example of the means of breaking free from the bondage of this type of soul-tie, which often develops in family situations. He broke a strong soul-tie by refusing and resisting the draw of the luxurious life of Pharaoh's court. In fact, he took a bold and risky stand against it:

> By faith Moses, when he was come to years, refused to be called the son of Pharaoh's daughter.
>
> Heb. 11:24

This must have been a difficult decision for him, because he no doubt loved and respected his "mother" and would not

91

have desired to cause her pain. It was necessary, however, for his growth and freedom in God.

Submission To ESP,
Hypnotism Or Divination

Soul-ties can be created by allowing oneself to be hypnotized, or permitting someone to "practice" ESP or fortune-telling upon us. We have encountered numerous severely tormented individuals who had been the victims of hypnotism, and more commonly ESP. Usually Extrasensory Perception (ESP) is either a form of drug-related witchcraft, or a merely a cover for overt witchcraft.

God designed Adam (and all subsequent mankind) with an inherent defense mechanism against demonization, which is called *willpower*. Man can elect to voluntarily lower the drawbridge of his mind by allowing someone to hypnotize him, or to practice ESP on him. This doorway to his soul can be opened through illegal drugs, through fear or simply through voluntary submission to a stronger individual. Nonetheless, man has the power to refuse to allow his mind (soul) to be violated. Even if in the past his mind has been violated by demonic intrusion, or by the presence of soul-ties, Jesus still wills for such captives to be free!

Souls Bound (-Tied)
With an Oath or Vow

Making promises and commitments is part of everyday life. However, in more serious cases, we must make note to break the soul-ties created in vows or promises if we realize that the vows we have made cannot be kept.

The subject of vows is little understood, but is extremely important, especially for the Christian.

> ...Then her vows shall stand, and her bonds wherewith she **bound her soul** shall stand.
>
> Num. 30:7b

ॐ Scripture uses here the Hebrew word, '*acar*, pronounced aw-sar. It has a root meaning "to yoke or hitch;" with alternate illuminating renderings, "to fasten in any sense, as in bind, fast, hold, keep, imprison, put in bonds, tie."

> Better is it that thou **shouldest not vow**, than that thou shouldest vow and not pay. **Suffer not thy mouth to cause thy flesh to sin...**
>
> Eccl. 5:5–6a

Vows are extremely serious, and are taken far more seriously by heaven than by modern man. The following rather lengthy passages from Numbers 30 are included in their entirety because they are not well known and are extremely important for spiritual warfare, and are especially significant for the breaking of spiritual bondages of the soul!

> And Moses spake... saying, This is the thing which the LORD hath commanded. **If a man vow a vow unto the LORD, or swear an oath to bind his soul with a bond; he shall not break his word, he shall do according to all that proceedeth out of his mouth.**
>
> Num. 30:1-2

The significance of this passage cannot be ignored: if a man swears an oath, or makes a vow, his soul is bound to the completion or fulfillment of that to which he has sworn or vowed, and there are no exceptions noted.

A related principle, and a beautiful revelation, is that God binds Himself by His words:

> My covenant will I not break, nor alter the thing that is gone out of my lips.
>
> Ps. 89:34

Man, likewise, binds himself with his words. A commitment to God or to another man is created by a vow or a promise. This is probably one of the reasons for the Lord's warning or admonition:

> But let your communication be, Yea, yea; Nay, nay: for whatsoever is more than these cometh of evil.
>
> Matt. 5:37

> A fool's mouth is his destruction, and his lips are the snare of his soul.
>
> Prov. 18:7

Man is instructed simply to say, "Yes" for yes and "No" for no!

Notice the difference between the vows made by a man, and the vows made by a woman:

Also if a woman makes a vow to the LORD, and binds herself by an obligation in her father's house in her youth, and her father hears her vow and her obligation by which she has bound herself, and her father says nothing to her, **then all her vows shall stand** and every obligation by which she has bound herself shall stand. But if her father should forbid her on the day he hears of it, **none of her vows or her obligations by which she has bound herself shall stand**; and the LORD will forgive her because her father had forbidden her. However, if she should marry while under her vows or the rash statement of her lips by which she has bound herself, and her husband hears of it and says nothing to her on the day he hears it, then **her vows shall stand** and her obligations by which she has bound herself shall stand. "But if on the day her husband hears of it, he forbids her, then **he shall annul her vow** which she is under and the rash statement of her lips by **which she has bound herself**; and the LORD will forgive her.

Num. 30:3–8 NASB

From this section we can plainly see that the woman who isn't in her right mind, or who isn't thinking clearly, can have her erratic actions undone by the one in authority over her. For example if she says, "I wish I were dead" or prays "God, please kill me now," the husband can renounce and revoke her request, or vow.

Note the salient points in the passage. If the woman is still under the authority of her father, then her father has the authority to revoke her vow, to prevent her coming under bondage, and to cause the Lord's forgiveness to flow to her. If she is married, then her husband in like fashion has authority over her to break the vow or oath's effect, to make it null and void.

But every vow of a widow, and of her that is divorced, wherewith they have bound their souls, shall stand against her.

Num. 30:9

Unfortunately, under this Old Covenant law, the widow and the divorced woman do not have anyone to set aside their vows. The vows which they make shall stand, until or unless, one should come with the power to break them.

Not to be overlooked is the clear statement in verse eight of this chapter, that unless the father or husband intervenes in her behalf, the woman has bound her soul! Her soul will remain in such bondage, until someone comes on the scene with the authority and power and loving concern to break her bondage. Praise be to God, a Greater One has come, in the person of Jesus Christ, who possesses such authority, power and love!

This enforcement of this revelation is repeated in Numbers 30:

Every vow, and every binding oath to afflict the soul, her husband may establish it, or her husband may make it void.

Num. 30:13

Once again notice both the clear statement and the responsibility placed upon the husband, to both hear and set aside the vow, or to allow it to be established. This foreshadows the tremendous authority later granted by Jesus to believers in Matthew 18:

> At the same time came the disciples unto Jesus... Verily I say unto you, Whatsoever ye shall bind on earth shall be bound in heaven: and whatsoever ye shall loose on earth shall be loosed in heaven.
>
> Matt. 18:1a, 18

The literal meaning of this passage in Matthew 18, because of its tense, should read, "whatsoever you bind on earth is already bound in heaven," and "whosoever you loose on earth has already been loosed in heaven."

How can this possibly be? It is true and possible only because it is the Holy Spirit who leads us, either to bind or to loosen, in accordance with the will of God. Thus our actions parallel that which has already been done in the heavenly realm.

Jesus gave His disciples the authority to both bind and loose from bondages, in much the same way that the father or husband of the woman could set aside or break her bondages. Thus, the disciples were empowered to break, or set aside, the bondages which the potential *Bride of Christ* might experience!

The Bridegroom, Jesus, has placed us in the role of husbands and fathers to void the self-destructive wishes, intentions and deceptions that may afflict the Bride of Christ. In fact, Jesus was the One who came with a greater anointing than that of the father or husband to set free those who were in bondage without a kinsman redeemer to act on their behalf, or to set them free. He announced at the commencement of His ministry:

> The Spirit of the Lord is upon me, because he hath anointed me to preach the gospel to the poor; he hath sent me to heal the brokenhearted, **to preach deliverance to the captives**, and recovering of sight to the blind, to set at liberty them that are bruised...
>
> Luke 4:18

These captives of whom He speaks actually are, as the literal Greek states, *prisoners-of-war*. How appropriate that phraseology is. From the standpoint of spiritual warfare and deliverance, that is exactly what these captives are — Satan's prisoners held in chains of bondage!

> ...in humility correcting those who are in opposition, if God perhaps will grant them repentance, so that they may know the truth, and that they may come to their senses and escape the **snare of the devil**, having been taken captive by him **to do his will**.
>
> 2 Tim. 2:25–26 NKJV

The NKJV renders the last clause of this passage as "taken captive to do his will." This translation is extremely revealing about the operation of the spiritual realm. It shows that Satan has snares for the people of God; that he desires (it is his will) to take captives. The servants of the Lord are to gently teach (i.e. without condemnation), instructing with meekness, those who "oppose themselves," who work against their own best interests.

There are two aspects, or possible interpretations, of this verse. The first, with which we are most familiar, would normally interpret it to mean, we "are held captive by Satan to prevent us from serving in the army of God, or from being able to do the will of God."

The second is suggested by the NKJV, which points to the other extreme, and Satan's greater goal, of "having the captives literally come into his service, to actually do his bidding." There are, of course, some who are so deluded by Satan's various wiles that they do come to a point of serving him; some of those even consciously draw upon or invoke his power. However, others are unaware of whom they are serving, but nonetheless participate in his work.

SOUL-TIES OF ADDICTION

Addictions are other snares that create soul-ties. The person addicted to heroin or other drugs is an interesting caricature of someone under a soul-tie or bondage. That person is dependent upon the "friend" who can meet his or her "need." The individual who is hooked is more concerned with having his need met than he is about morality, or any other obligations which he may have either to man or to God. Those in extreme soul-tie bondages are similarly unable to break free from the "supplier" of their perceived needs. Although we are using drugs for the purpose of an illustration, there are many other sources of cravings, dependency and addiction, such as prescription drugs, cigarettes, alcohol, sex, sweets.

SOUL-TIES OF IDOLATRY

Is it possible for one's soul to be bound to an inanimate object, or to a non-human? Certainly, through attachments made to idols, animals or places.

Spiritual harlotry refers to those who are ungodly joined to idols and who go to places of idol worship. Of course, all negative soul-ties are by definition, demonic in nature. However, there are specific soul-ties that can directly occur with demons.

Man who violates God's commandment and chooses to worship false gods, invites a demonic soul-tie with that idol, or the god (demon) that it represents.

> Thou shalt have no other gods before me.   Ex. 20:3

> Rather, that the things which the Gentiles sacrifice they sacrifice to demons and not to God, and I do not want you to have **fellowship with demons**.
>   1 Cor. 10:19–20 NKJV

Paul clearly warns that to sacrifice to an idol is to sacrifice to the devil (demon) behind the idol, or represented by the idol; and to do so is having fellowship with demons. This is a distinct warning to avoid demonic soul-ties.

In the blatantly occult workings of witchcraft, witches voluntarily bind themselves to demons, or bind demons to themselves, in order to gain greater power. We have delivered women from witchcraft who have bound themselves to Pan and similar demons by fire, smoke or blood in order to gain the power and protection against stronger demons whom they feared.

Similarly we have encountered children whose parents dedicated their souls to idols of gods and goddesses (demons) by sacrifices of smoke (incense), food or flowers placed upon altars or shrines. The babies were placed upon the altar and smoke blown across the child, dedicating the child to various Hindu or Buddhist idols. The effects upon the children are often both dramatic and tragic. The child so dedicated may be deformed, crippled, blinded, or unable to speak. We have rejoiced to see children delivered from such bondages when a parent repents and seeks deliverance for his child in Jesus' name.

Man may become attached in his soul to things. Thus idolatry occurs in various forms: to animals, to people, to babies; anything given inordinate affection can become an idol. Even something good and designed by God such as Nehusthan (2 Kings 18:4), can become distorted in the perception of the beholder and become an idol. Likewise something can begin as a good soul-tie; marriage, a parent-child bonding, or a friendship like that of Jonathan and David. All can start well but can become perverted or restrictive, as in the case of a *little girl spirit* that prevents a woman from maturing emotionally.

☞ Some common soulish attachments include:

- Places: "I left my heart in San Francisco. I left a piece of me there." Unnatural, sentimental attachments to places leave one depressed, sad or melancholy when unable to return to that place. This is also true of situations, such as unnaturally long periods of grief, a holding on to the feeling of sadness, or a refusing to be comforted like Jacob.

> How long shall I take counsel in my soul, having sorrow in my heart daily?
>
> Ps. 13:2a

- Things, Inanimate Objects: "I love my rifle, my Corvette, my computer, my house, my lucky shirt."

- Animals: Any pets, doting on dogs, cat fetishes, horses, any out of balance emotions directed toward animals. All can think of someone who overly dotes on his or her pet(s). Someone who would spend thousands of dollars to save a stray kitten may be out of balance.

What we are considering is actually inordinate affection, which I thought was a unique concept and teaching of my own, but I found Paul mentioned it first.

> Set your affection on things above, not on things on the earth... Mortify therefore... **inordinate affection**, evil concupiscence, and covetousness, which is idolatry:
>
> Col. 3:2–3, 5

THE FEAR OF DEATH

The *fear of death* becomes a means of exercising control and creating unnatural dependence. This *fear of death* opens one to create soul-ties with the person(s) that alleviates that surging fear.

☞ Some obvious candidates for that unhealthy soul-tie role, even among otherwise discerning Christians are:

- doctors, chiropractors and other "health experts"
- attorneys
- pastors

Additional possible candidates more likely to be employed by the undiscerning, or non-Christian, are:
- gurus, and leaders of cults
- psychics
- occult practitioners

A fear is often implanted that implies the person cannot live, financially or physically, without the assistance of the controller.

A variation on this *fear of death spirit* is the fear of causing the death of the controller. A parent may use the fear of death as a weapon, "If you don't do this for me, it will kill me." "You may kill me by moving away." "It would kill me if you..."

Fear of death causes the common ailment of insecurity. A small child depends on an adult for his or her very life. When the adult is undependable or inconsistent in his or her behavior, the child can easily come to *fear for his life*.

☞ This fear translates into adult insecurity and is evidenced by many kinds of torments:

- anxiety in any new situation

- embarrassment

- fear of rejection

- fear of the future, disease, poverty, disasters

- nervousness

An adult friend, mate or other authority figure may enter the scene who offers security through acceptance, worldly knowledge or spiritual counsel. This person can serve as a positive soul-tie leading the insecure one to the True Companion who "will stick closer than a brother," Jesus. If however, this individual seeks only to control the other, or does not refuse his or her over-dependency, then the insecure person, motivated by fear, becomes bound to another in an unhealthy way.

God is love. In love we find the answer for fear, as Jesus so often said, "Fear Not!" And Scripture reminds us: *If God be for us, who can be against us?* (Rom. 8:31b).

> There is no fear in love; but perfect love casteth out fear: because **fear hath torment**.
>
> 1 John 4:18a

The man who has been freed of the fear of death can face anything...

> And they overcame him by the blood of the Lamb, and by the word of their testimony; and they loved not their lives unto the death.
>
> Rev. 12:11

ATTEMPTED MANIPULATION THROUGH
A THREAT OF SUICIDE

This weapon of the *fear of death* or *fear of loss*, and the accompanying witchcraft it brings with it, comes in a variety of disguises. In more than twenty-eight years of ministry, my wife and I have frequently encountered attempted manipulation and witchcraft from those wanting to usurp control over us, over our ministry or over our Christian businesses. We have had people try to put us in bondage to them in a variety of ways. One example of the bizarre ways in which witchcraft was attempted against us was the case of Ella.

Mary, a longtime close spiritual friend who had received salvation and the Baptism in the Spirit in our prayer room, brought another woman, Ella, to see me at our Christian bookstore. Both of these women were in their late thirties. However, when they arrived, Ella was acting like a little lost puppy. I sensed that she was up to something and suggested that we go back into the warehouse where we could talk in complete privacy. Ella sat on a box of books, waiting like a plaintive zombie, as Mary began, "Poor Ella is extremely upset, and she has told me that if you won't hire her to work for you as a clerk in the bookstore, she will kill herself."

After a moment to catch my breath and recover from the shock of such blatant witchcraft and manipulation, I responded: "Come on, Mary... think for a minute of what you are saying. Obviously, I couldn't hire her on that basis. If I asked her to do something she didn't want to do, she'd just threaten to kill herself. Besides, you know that this is witchcraft." Had we given in to this, Ella would have established a tie with our souls stemming from our fear of her instability.

Mary paled, gasped, and blurted out, "Oh, my gosh you're right; this is witchcraft. You shouldn't hire her under any circumstances."

Today, twenty years later, Mary is still counseling and ministering deliverance in her church, yet, even she was sucked in by Ella's story. Witchcraft can be very subtle and compelling and may even sound logical at first. This is another reason that the Lord in His wisdom has provided the supernatural gift of *discerning of spirits* (1 Cor. 12:10) and admonishes us to *try the spirits* (1 John 4:1) to see whether they are really of God.

> ...he that is spiritual judgeth all things...
>
> 1 Cor. 2:15a

SOUL-TIES OF GRIEF

In many cases, harmful and unhealthy adult soul-ties develop through the death of a loved one, a close friend or a relative. This is especially true if the death was sudden and unexpected, or if the individual battling the soul-tie was present at the time of death.

Unnatural grief is often rooted in feelings of guilt. It is expressed in the thought life as, "somehow I should have done something more for the deceased," or "Perhaps I might have prevented the death." Suicide almost always affects the survivors in this fashion. The normal period of grief can last from weeks to a year or two. Caution should be taken against any unnatural grief which lasts longer than that, lest it develop into a soul-tie with the dead party. If not dealt with in a timely manner, there will almost always be a spirit of death, death-wish or suicide that comes upon the grieving survivor.

Soul-ties can be created with dead relatives through bondages of obligation, or bondages of fear. For example, seeing grandpa in his coffin, or being forced to kiss him goodbye at his wake may bring recurring nightmares, or visitations at night.

Most of us have heard stories of ancestors who died of "heartbreak" upon losing a child, or some other tragedy. This can still happen today. Excessive or prolonged grief leads to heaviness, despair, heartbreak, and death. Soul-ties of grief with a deceased loved one often manifest with symptoms of pain in the area of the heart, and may be mistaken for symptoms of heart attacks.

Many ministers have encountered this type of soul-tie in women who have had abortions. They have a soul-tie of guilt with their deceased child and often overcompensate by vehemently or violently opposing abortion.[3] The unconfronted spirits of abortion frequently open these women to other death spirits, such as murderous hate or suicide.

Sometimes a soul-tie with the dead can develop into a sort of "communion" with the dead person, feeling the person's presence, or seeing them repeatedly in dreams or visions. On one occasion a young woman, a full-blooded Native American, came for deliverance. During the session, her deceased Hopi grandfather spoke and chanted through his granddaughter as we ministered deliverance to her. She shared with us that she had been taught to revere her grandfather who had been a tribal witch doctor, and thus a soul-tie had formed.

It is not uncommon for demons to manifest as deceased relatives. They may masquerade as the relative to deceive, as in a

---

[3] I have written a book on the subject, *Ministering to Abortion's Aftermath*. Available at www.impactchristianbooks.com

séance, or to promote belief in reincarnation. Or, they manifest during deliverance when the spirit of the relative or ancestor has been passed down. If the curse and the accountability for the sins of the ancestor can be passed down for generations, it should not surprise us to find that demons of those personalities can be passed down as well.

On another occasion a young male college student came for deliverance. He shared in my prayer room that he was barely able to function. He explained that he went to school in the morning and hid behind the racks of books in the library until it was time to go home. "I don't think that is a normal way for a college student to act," he concluded.

I agreed. We began delivering him of demonic spirits. At one point his grandmother spoke through him in her voice. It was clearly the voice of an old lady, not that of the young man. Later, his mother also spoke through him in her voice, as did several aunts. There were numerous apparent soul-ties that had allowed these entities to enter his personality, meaning his soul. When he first came for help, he appeared to be somewhat effeminate, which should not have been surprising with the female entities within him. He had failed to resist the strong female influences in his life, through laziness or fear, and also through, in his case, preexisting inherited spirits. Often we let other people run our lives and make decisions for us, even though we realize we should be making such decisions for ourselves.

In several sessions, we cast about two hundred spirits out of him, and he later told me that he cast out another six hundred at home on his own. Today he is married, the father of several children, and is active in his church.

These two cases illustrate several obvious door openers for soul-ties and demonic intrusion: reverence, fear, awe, or worship of another person, dependency on another, or simply refusing to assume responsibility for oneself. The young Native American girl had been taught to revere her grandfather, the witchdoctor, and thus a door was opened for spirits; the young man allowed himself to remain dependent, and to idolize the female figures in his life. Worship of anyone or anything other than Jesus Christ is a serious door opener.

Super-Spirituality Manipulation

Super-spirituality manipulation is practiced by an individual in the church, or outside it, who professes to be more spiritual than others (i.e., you), who claims to have a close relationship with God and to hear from Him regularly and directly with guidance for others. (Note that this is not very logical: whom is God most likely to speak to about "you" but you?) Recognize that false prophets give false words from the Lord.

A Soul-Tie Can Exist With Oneself

When a young child suffers the actual or perceived loss of a parent, or feels that the love of the parent has been lost, a soul-tie can develop with himself. These conditions may arise through death, divorce, illness, prolonged separation, being ignored or rejected, hospital stays, etc.

The result is the accepting of a *little girl* or *boy spirit*, which reflects a stunting of the emotional growth, and an internal soul-tie with either a portion of herself that existed before the time of loss, or the creating of either an imaginary, idealized child who is happy and loved, or an idealized parent to fill the void in her life.

The real child lives in a state of grief because of her separation from that ideal happy child, and the idealized absent parent. The functioning is very similar to that of a soul-tie with an actual person.

The little girls involved, or boys, are often reluctant to grow up and face responsibilities. *They seem to feel if they can remain a child, or child-like, they will be excused from the difficult parts of life and people won't expect too much of them.* They simply remain dependent. However, dependency is also one of the key invitations to soul-ties, so such children are especially vulnerable.

In severe cases the child may create more than one "alter-ego" and even give them names by which to identify them and differentiate between them. These are referred to as multiple personalities or "alters." We have seen them cast out, resulting in dramatic changes. [4] Remember, demons seek to fragment the soul of an individual from the time of his or her conception.

> O LORD my God, in thee do I put my trust: save me from all them that persecute me, and **deliver me:** Lest he **tear my soul** like a lion, **rending it in pieces,** while there is none to deliver.
>
> Ps. 7:1–2

This passage not only indicates the distinct danger of a soul being torn into pieces and fragmented, but also indicates the solution to the problem, **deliverance!**

---

[4] A letter which is particularly illustrative of the soul-tie element in multiple personalities is reproduced in the appendix.

When Satan removes or arranges the removing of a piece of the soul, he does so for a reason: to replace that vacated area with something else, a demon (cf. Eph. 4:27). This is another wile or method employed by the enemy in gaining a "place" within the individual. He would love to so bind an individual with soul-ties that he is unable to respond to the Lord's call, or to feel ineligible or disqualified to respond.

SATAN PERVERTS GODLY SOUL-TIES

Unfortunately, we frequently hear of the downfall of ministers through sexual sins. What we have discovered with regard to soul-ties helps in understanding and explaining this prevalent phenomenon. When any man attempts to help a woman, or when a minister counsels a young divorcee, soul-ties often form. On the woman's part there may be soul-ties of dependency and of looking to the one who is providing assistance and godly wisdom as her male counterpart, or head, fulfilling the role voided by her absent husband. There are other factors but this serves to illustrate her potential vulnerability.

On the male part, there can be a familial soul-tie as that of a father to daughter, brother to sister, pastor to member, teacher to pupil, or that of friend to friend. These are all godly forms of relationship. However, if the man and especially the pastor, is not on guard (and is unfamiliar with the potential dangers of soul-ties) he is vulnerable to crossing the line. If he does, he allows these godly relationships to become something distorted. The danger is that the loving *spiritual* ties which already exist may merge into *carnal*. Then the friend-to-friend tie becomes a lover-to-lover tie. A knowledge of soul-ties helps us to be on guard against crossing the line. To be forewarned is to be forearmed.

Pastor Win Worley encountered and cast out a spirit that identified itself as a "good soul-tie breaker." Satan opposes and seeks to destroy all good soul-ties, especially those in marriage, or within the Body of Christ. Pastor Worley observed that there were seven spirits that seemed to be in subjection to and working with the "good soul-tie breaking spirit." Among them were fear of rejection, fear of hurt, deception, dependency, mistrust, hate, and jealousy.

As we have seen, through the reality of negative soul-ties, and through the inappropriate choices we make in relationships such as misplaced affection, we enter into deep-rooted bondage. Perhaps you are not sure if you have fallen into one of the traps which have been mentioned. In the next chapter we will describe symptoms commonly experienced by those ensnared in unhealthy soul-ties. Use this information as a diagnostic tool to evaluate the condition of your own soul.

4

SIDE-EFFECTS OF UNHEALTHY SOUL-TIES

The symptoms negative soul-links produce underscore the urgency of defining the unhealthy soul-ties that may exist in one's life, and the necessity of being free from them.

☞ When one is tied to the wrong person, certain common side effects are observed. They will include some of the following:

- *Loss of individuality and self-confidence.*
  Tendency to think of oneself in terms of relationship to someone else, accompanied by inferiority and a lack of competence.

- *Loss of clear thinking in decision making.*

   Double-mindedness, the inability or shirking from decision making.

- *Loss of peace*

   The presence of fear, worry, anxiety, or nervousness especially around other people; feeling of being pressured, or under stress to always please the other person.

- *Loss of the ability to really love others.*

   The presence of anger and resentment.

- *Loss of spiritual liberty and personal freedom.*

   Accompanied by guilt and condemnation and by feelings of being smothered or constantly restrained.

   In addition, a person who has become vulnerable to the control of his acquaintances will also develop added vulnerability to more evil soul-ties. He will find himself developing relationship problems with other acquaintances.

- *Loss of good health accompanied by infirmity.*

   Soul-ties of susceptibility to sickness or affliction may be inherited along with an ancestral soul-tie, often seen as a generational curse or spirit. Such ungodly soul-ties of sickness can exist alongside

114

the godly soul-ties within a marriage, until cast out. For example my wife, Sue, experienced hair loss and fear of cancer after I had cancer because of her deep feelings for me. She became vulnerable through me.

It is readily observable that people who are bound by anger, fear, anxiety, and other emotional dysfunctions resulting from being inordinately controlled, become susceptible to disease.

And, of course, the most grievous side-effect,

• *Loss of closeness to the Father*

This has all sorts of disastrous consequences, including obstacles and impediments to our walk with God, hardening our hearts toward God, shutting out the Lord's voice in our daily lives, and erecting a wall between us and ministry of the Holy Spirit.

HOW DO I KNOW IF ANOTHER IS ATTEMPTING TO GAIN CONTROL OVER MY SOUL?

There are a few "gut-checks" that we can make in order to diagnose whether we are coming under control of another person.

☞ For instance, one may notice that

- Someone else makes decisions or plans for your life

- Someone else is being overly protective of you

- Someone else is being threatened by any new friendships you make

- Someone is exercising financial control over you – parents, bosses, debt.

In more extreme cases, you will find that someone has thoughts of harm commingled with thoughts of control. As the following Scripture makes clear, it is definitely possible for a mere man, motivated by evil, to do at least five things:

> For ye suffer, **if a man bring you into bondage,** if a man devour you, if a man take of you, if a man exalt himself, if a man smite you on the face.
>
> 2 Cor. 11:20

These five things that those with evil intentions can do are:

1. Bring you into bondage;

2. Devour you, following the pattern of Satan, the "roaring lion seeking whom he may devour." Thus, this individual is doing Satan's work and is his agent;

3. Take from you that which is yours (wrong you, rob you of reputation, things, or your wife);

4. Exalt himself over you, thus putting you down;

5. Smite you, strike you, or hurt you, physically or emotionally.

Any or all of these may cause you to suffer, but Jesus wants to set you free from all such bondage and from its resultant suffering. That's one of the main reasons that He came... *to set the captives free*!

OBSESSIVE THOUGHT LIFE

Another side-effect of an unhealthy soul-tie is an obsessive thought life. This is often characterized by a feeling of compulsion to be with or to see another person — e.g. "I can't forget her!"; "I can't get her out of my mind!"

The thought life consists of both the conscious and the unconscious.

Conscious Thought Life: where one is plagued with memories or thoughts of the other party, including fantasies or daydreams (not necessarily sexual fantasies, but they often seem to have a sexual aspect).

Unconscious Thought Life: dreams, nightmares, terrors. Individuals often complain about being unable to get the other person out of their thoughts or dreams. They may be tormented with nightmares or night terrors about the other party running their life, controlling them or even killing them.

What Do You Fear?

As mentioned, fear can be the stronghold, and the stranglehold, behind ungodly soul-ties. A strong presence of fear is a common side-effect of unhealthy relationships. It has been validly said that "the thing which we fear tends to become our God."

By the same token, anything that serves to remove our fear can also become our God. Thus, we find many people worshiping and making an idol of money, which removes or alleviates the fear of poverty; or worshiping doctors, who alleviate their fear of sickness, disease or death. Jesus should be our Source and the One to whom we look when fear attacks us:

> Thus saith the LORD; **Cursed be the man that trusteth in man,** and maketh flesh his arm, and whose heart departeth from the LORD.
>
> Jer. 17:5

This Scripture makes it clear that looking to another source, any other source, especially man, is to depart from the Lord. This is a thought echoed in numerous Scriptures, such as...

> It is better to trust in the LORD than to put confidence in man. It is better to trust in the LORD than to put confidence in princes.
>
> Ps. 118:8–9

At the heart of many evil soul-ties is some kind of fear. Scripture places the fear of death as the greatest controlling force in people's lives. Hebrews states:

Therefore, since the children share in flesh and blood, He Himself likewise also partook of the same, that through death He might render powerless him who had the power of death, that is, the devil, and might free those who **through fear of death were subject to slavery all their lives.**

Heb. 2:14–15

☞ Remember, when you become linked to another for ungodly reasons, you become susceptible to not only all the symptoms previously mentioned, but you may also acquire demonic problems from the dominant individual, including their faithlessness and rebellion. *You might even find yourself seeking to control another just as you have been controlled.*

The bottom line is evil soul-ties must be broken. The next chapter will outline the steps to freedom.

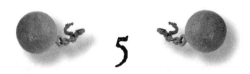

THE CURE:
BREAKING SOUL-TIES

Virtually all battles with Satan are fought upon the battlefield located in the mind. This is true with regard to deliverance in general, and breaking of soul-ties in particular. The candidate for freedom must come to recognize that a soul-tie problem exists, make the decision that he or she wants to be free, and then determine to take steps in that direction.

These steps will include some or all of the following: confessing, renouncing, verbally breaking soul-ties, casting out evil spirits, and then calling back the fragmented portions of the soul that it might be restored and healed.

Force yourself, if necessary, to heed advice and to renew your mind, as Paul recommends in Philippians 4. Often, when under the sway of soul-tie domination, the individual is totally blinded to the control exercised over him. He may go from pastor to pastor, counselor to counselor, seeking agreement for what he wants to believe.

> And be not conformed to this world: but be ye transformed by the renewing of your mind
>
> Rom. 12:2

There are varying degrees of difficulty in breaking soul-ties. Normally soul-ties are not formed overnight. The degree of difficulty encountered in breaking a soul-tie will usually be affected by the duration and strength of that relationship. Soul-ties from relationships presumed to be rooted in love, involving sexual contact, and those rooted in fear or the occult are usually the strongest and most difficult for the victim to break. However, even simple over-dependence upon a mother can be very strong if allowed to exist for a long time.

> And ye shall know the truth, and the truth shall make you free.
>
> John 8:32

> If the Son therefore shall make you free, ye shall be free indeed.
>
> John 8:36

KNOWLEDGE OF SOUL-TIES

Arm yourself with knowledge. Ignorance or *lack of awareness* was the doorway for these unhealthy soul-ties to gain a stronghold, so the obvious solution is knowledge through education. We must educate ourselves as to their existence and effects. This learning process includes not only studying material on the subject, but learning to pattern our relationships after the perfect example of Jesus Himself.

Jesus avoided all control from every other source, except God the Father, and He resisted all temptations to sin. Holiness requires the need to sacrifice temporary pleasure for the greater goal of personal and spiritual freedom. We need also to learn the tactics and wiles of the enemy.

Adam broke faith with God by disobedience. He failed to keep (literally "guard") the Garden because of his lack of knowledge of Satan's intentions. What were the devil's intentions? They were to gain control over Adam and all of God's creation, which had been entrusted to Adam. Isaiah states Satan's intentions:

> For thou hast said in thine heart, I will ascend into heaven, I will exalt my throne above the stars of God:
>
> I will sit also upon the mount of the congregation, in the sides of the north: I will ascend above the heights of the clouds; I will be like the most High.
>
> Isa. 14:13-14

Jesus, the last Adam, successfully resisted Satan's attempt to control Him, and thereby set the pattern for us to be free!

> Again, the devil taketh him up into an exceeding high mountain, and showeth him all the kingdoms of the world, and the glory of them; And saith unto him, All these things will I give thee, if thou wilt fall down and worship me. Then saith Jesus unto him, Get thee hence, Satan: for it is written, Thou shalt worship the Lord thy God, and him only shalt thou serve. Then the devil leaveth him, and, behold, angels came and ministered unto him.
>
> Matt. 4:8-11

DISAGREEMENT WITH UNHEALTHY SOUL-TIES

Agreement is the second major factor in the formulation of wrongful soul-ties, and the obvious antidote is disagreement.

Herein lays the difficulty. In most cases disagreement may require cutting off as many aspects of the controlling relationships — at least until the person being controlled becomes able to walk in freedom and to think for himself. For instance, in the case of a controlling parent exercising influence over an adult son or daughter, decisions about career paths and how to raise your children may be two areas of attempted unhealthy influence that need to be cut off. This should include divesting oneself of certain gifts or "hooks" from the controller. Some relationships may take years to be restored because the controlling party will not be willing to recognize or acknowledge the freedom of the other person.

The most difficult problems arise when the controller is a family member or an employer with whom you may not be able to totally sever all ties. One helpful suggestion is to rethink the definitions of family, church, and citizenship. Again using Jesus as our pattern, we are reminded of His words:

> Who is my mother? and who are my brethren?.. For whosoever shall do the will of my Father which is in heaven, the same is **my brother, and sister, and mother.**
>
> Matt. 12:48a, 50

> He that loveth father or mother more than me is not worthy of me: and he that loveth son or daughter more than me is not worthy of me.
>
> Matt. 10:37

The promise in Romans 8 is that the Holy Spirit will bring us to our true Father (Abba). We become adopted into the family of God the Father, when we receive God's Son, Jesus Christ, as our Savior.

> For both He who sanctifies and those who are sanctified are all from one Father; for which reason He is not ashamed to call them brethren...
> Heb. 2:11 NASB

> But as many as received him, to them gave he power to become the **sons of God**, even to them that believe on his name...
> John 1:12

We also need to redefine the meaning of the church. Jesus defined the church by its locality, e.g. the church of Ephesus or Smyrna, not recognizing what we today call denominations. Paul acknowledged an elder or bishop as one of several leaders over an entire geographic area, and argued in First Corinthians 3:3-7 against carnal division based upon personalities.

> For while one saith, I am of Paul; and another, I am of Apollos: are ye not carnal?
> 1 Cor. 3:4

Although we may subdivide for the sake of convenience, we are still part of the one Body in any spiritual locality, and part of the one universal Body. We are now citizens of a heavenly city and our allegiance is to the Ruler of that city.

In other words, the second key to freedom for our souls is

to change our way of thinking; to *fall out of agreement* with all that attempts to hold us to wrong allegiances. It is only when we become free and independent in Christ that we can become a blessing to another. This battle is first fought in the mind, and must be won on that battlefield.

Scripture makes it clear that in certain circumstances, it is necessary to withdraw, or remove oneself from a situation:

> Perverse disputings of men of corrupt minds, and destitute of the truth, supposing that gain is godliness: **from such withdraw thyself.**
>
> 1 Tim. 6:5

> In the last days... men shall be... having a form of godliness, but denying the power thereof: **from such turn away.**
>
> 2 Tim. 3:1,2,5

Satan seems to fight more determinedly against our achieving freedom from wrongful soul-ties than against any other kind of deliverance. This is because it is easier to cast out a demon than to cast out a person we can see. No human being is either all good or entirely evil. Just about the time we begin our "flight to freedom," the one to whom we are tied redefines himself or herself as loving and needy. Feelings of guilt and selfishness creep over us, and we must resist being drawn back into old patterns of bondage.

Before freedom can be accomplished in the spiritual realm, we need to be absolutely convinced of the necessity of breaking the tie no matter how the controlling party subsequently behaves, because that party will most likely "pull out all the stops." We must also determine not to be controlled by a fear of the pain of burning bridges. Remember that the less you are controlled by another, the more you will be able to yield yourself to God's control.

Next we need to realize that a wrongful soul-tie functions like an invisible chain holding our spirits down. The final solution is spiritual and is won with prayer. The following steps will be helpful.

STEPS TO FREEDOM AND VICTORY

1) *Forgive All Others*

> And when ye stand praying, **forgive**, if ye have aught against any, that your Father also which is in heaven may forgive you.
>
> Mark 11:25

Forgiveness has played an essential part in more than 90% of the deliverances we have ministered over the last twenty-eight years. Unforgiveness maintains and reinforces the soul-tie. It also prevents God from aiding the freedom seeker. In a certain sense, His hands are tied, for His own Word declares the governing principle:

> And his lord was wroth, and delivered him to the tormentors, till he should pay all that was due unto him. So likewise shall my heavenly Father do also unto you, if ye from your hearts forgive not everyone his brother their trespasses.
>
> Matt. 18:34–35

One should become familiar with the steps to forgiveness given in the "Forgiveness Teaching" section in *Power for Deliverance: Songs of Deliverance*, available through Impact Christian Books (www.impactchristianbooks.com). The candidate should pray a simple prayer from his heart, forgiving all who he thinks have wronged him, such as the following:

Lord Jesus, I come to you now confessing my unforgiveness as sin. I renounce all sins involved in my harboring unforgiveness against _____ and _____. I give up my right to be angry with them, and, by a decision of my will, I forgive them for wronging me, and I ask you to forgive them as well. Amen!

☞ Note: *Forgiveness* is not the same as *Trust*.

There will always be resentment, whether conscious or not, against the one who has snared your soul. How do we reconcile those feelings?

If we look at an extreme case, it would be possible to respect a woman as your mother, and to acknowledge her for having given you birth, even if she was, or has since become, a prostitute. In the same way, we could separate her from her controlling demons. Remember the old adage: We must forgive the sinner, but not necessarily the sin.

For example, if the neighbor's dog bites you and the neighbor then asks you to forgive him for the incident, you can validly forgive him. But that does not mean that you must expose yourself to his dog to be bitten again to prove it. If an employee steals from you and asks for forgiveness, you can forgive, but you would be foolish to leave the keys to the safe with that employee. Forgiveness does not mean an immediate restoration of trust. *Trust must be earned.*

Again, the adult who was wronged as a child by a parent can validly forgive the offending parent for the abuse involved, but need not expose himself to more abuse in order to prove that forgiveness. This is a common lie of the enemy. "If you have really forgiven, you wouldn't have any hesitation about going over there and spending time with that person."

There is another wise adage: "Once burned; twice shy." There is nothing wrong with exercising caution! For example, one would be wise not to allow a child to be in a room alone with a parent who has a history of molestation or sexual abuse. The parent's repentance for past behavior is one thing, proving himself trustworthy is an entirely different matter. If you experience a check in your spirit, or feel mistrust toward someone who has abused you in the past, heed that as a warning from the Lord, until He chooses to direct you otherwise with His peace.

2. Cut All Improper Soul-Ties

Just as an infant must have his umbilical cord cut if he is to survive in the physical world, the Christian must have his soul-ties severed so that he can survive and grow in the spiritual realm. A prayer to break soul-ties would go along the lines of:

I make the decision now to break all unnatural authority, manipulation, domination, or control, exercised over me by _____, _____ or _____ . I renounce all covenants, pacts, promises, curses, and every other work of darkness to which I have been exposed or made liable by my own actions or the actions of others. As a volitional act and by the decision of my own will, I loose myself from every soul-tie and from every form of bondage of my soul or body to Satan, or any of his agents be they human or demonic. I choose also to now present my body to the Lord as a living sacrifice, as the Scripture recommends, and to walk in holiness as You, Lord Jesus, enable me to do so.

Amen

③ *Restore the Fragmented Soul*

Counter-attack and have as a goal to replace the damaged soul with a whole soul, to cast out the evil spirits and to replace them with good spirits from God such as the *fruit of the Spirit*. If the person has been tormented with fear, pray for them to be filled with peace.

One should pray for the fragmented soul to be made complete, and totally restored. This will include closing the door of dependence.

Thus one may be led to *call back* the fragmented parts of the soul, or heart. In doing so, use a prayer such as the following.

In the name of Jesus Christ, I command every portion of my soul that has been fragmented, torn or broken, to come back into its proper place; to be healed; every piece of my heart to be returned; my soul to be restored and every bondage or related soul-tie to be completely broken. Lord, now I ask you to heal my soul, and to bind up my broken heart. I ask you to guard my heart going forward by Your power, Your strength and Your love. Please keep my heart and mind pure, free without strings attached, through Christ Jesus.

Amen

4. Confess Any Remaining Sins

Take a moment, and spend some time with the Lord. Today is a very special day. You are conducting a transaction today with Jesus: you are giving him all your regrets, the things that make you feel bad about yourself, and He is taking them from you — forever! And as a blessing, He is going to wash you as white as snow.

I prayerfully confess now to You, Lord Jesus, that I have sinned by doing _____, _____ and _____. I recognize these were wrong and I am sorry for them, please forgive me for _____ and _____, and wash all sin and guilt from me with Your blood – make me as white as snow. I accept and receive your merciful forgiveness, and will do all in my power to walk in righteousness, with Your help.

Amen

5. *Pray and Take Authority to Cast out Any Spirits*

Cast out possible spirits of lust, perversions, addiction, occult control, anger, resentment, hate, guilt or fear.

> And these signs shall follow them that believe; in my name
> **they shall cast out devils.**
>
> Mark 16:17a

God has invested unbelievable power and authority in you to cast out every evil spirit and to break every demonic bondage. You are a believer, the power is yours!

> Whatsoever ye shall bind on earth **shall be bound in heaven:** and whatsoever ye shall loose on earth **shall be loosed in heaven...** if two of you shall agree on earth as touching any thing that they shall ask, **it shall be done for them** of my Father which is in heaven.
>
> Matt. 18:18–20

> Behold, **I give unto you power...** over all the power of the enemy: and nothing shall by any means hurt you.
>
> Luke 10:19

Having done the previous steps, now use the authority given to you and the privilege of invoking the Name of Jesus — command each spirit by name, to leave you right now in Jesus' Name!

In the name of Jesus Christ, I take authority over the spirit(s) tormenting me. I bind you, you spirit of _____ and I break your hold over me. I command you to be defeated, your will to be broken and your strategy against me to be set into confusion and disarray. You leave me right now in Jesus' name!

Amen

6. Break Ungodly Vows with Prayer

We commit ourselves by our words. Pay special attention to the way you speak; some habits may need to be broken. Pray about such vows as:

- "I'll never do _____ again, Lord, if you'll just save me this time!"

- "I wish he (she, or I) were dead."

- "I'd give my right arm to..."

- "I'm dying for a smoke, a drink, a..."

- "If I'm not pregnant this time, I'll never have sex with Joe again."

- "I'll never be like my mother, father, boss, etc."

Such statements can become self-fulfilling curses, because they focus one's attention upon the evil, and reinforce a negative soul-tie with the one hated or resented. Each one who feels the need to renounce and break any vows which he has made, or may have unknowingly spoken in the past should break them, by praying a prayer like this:

In the name of Jesus Christ, I hereby renounce and revoke any vow that I have made in the past, whether made intentionally or unintentionally. I take back the words that I spoke when I said _____. I also break any soul-ties resulting from those vows and take authority over any evil spirits sent to enforce a particular vow to torment me. I command your will to be broken, your strategy to be sent into confusion, your plans to be finished, and to leave me right now in Jesus' name!

Amen

PREVENTING FURTHER HARMFUL SOUL-TIES

Overcoming condemnation means living a life of liberty instead of bondage. One must learn to recognize the difference between freedom and condemnation. The men and women described throughout this book were in bondage, as are all who are under unhealthy soul-ties. This ought not so to be. Remember,

> Now the Lord is that Spirit: and where the Spirit of the Lord is, **there is liberty**.
>
> 2 Cor. 3:17

Liberty, not bondage, is the Lord's heritage for His children. Which are you enjoying? Remember God's words to Pharaoh, *"Let my people go!"* God has not changed: that is still His will for His people.

LEARN TO AVOID DEPENDENCY

A healthy train of thought helps avoid dependency:

I am not vulnerable to you, because I do not fear you, nor will I be devastated by your rejection. More important, I am not going to become dependent upon you, or to you, because I have chosen to become, and remain, dependent only upon the Lord Jesus Christ. I belong to Him, and if He be for me what need I fear? I am accepted in the Beloved.

> So that we may boldly say, The Lord is my helper, and **I will not fear** what man shall do unto me.
>
> Heb. 13:6

RESIST THE DEVIL
OR ANYONE ELSE TRYING TO CONTROL YOU

What we have been considering so far deals with the first portion of James 4:7, submitting ourselves to God and changing masters.

> *"Submit yourselves therefore to God.* **Resist the devil and** he will flee from you."
>
> James 4:7

The next portion of the verse gives one of the most powerful keys to victory for all forms of warfare, the principle of *spiritual resistance*. To continue walking in freedom, one must resist.

If someone has exercised the power of control over you, if he has manipulated, dominated or exercised witchcraft against you, you must make the decision to *resist that power*. You do this by making a firm decision of your will to not be controlled.

In doing so, you make a decision to draw a line in the sand: to refuse to allow yourself to be vulnerable. This decision may include refusing to accept gifts, financial help or anything else which you determine has an ulterior motive, or a hidden hook included.

Remember the promise given in James 4:7; the devil will flee from you. Jesus has already defeated Satan. It is now up to us to experientially defeat him in the same way simply by applying the work that Jesus did. Just as we apply the blood to ourselves for salvation, we must apply the completed work of Calvary to defeat Satan's works of darkness and thereby walk in freedom and holiness.

> I beseech you therefore, brethren, by the mercies of God, that ye **present your bodies a living sacrifice**, holy, acceptable unto God, which is your reasonable service
>
> Rom. 12:1

> And the God of peace shall bruise Satan under your feet shortly, The grace of our Lord Jesus Christ be with you, Amen.
>
> Rom. 16:20

REPLACE IMPROPER SOUL-TIES

If a baby is separated from its mother at birth, it needs someone else to fill that void; someone else must provide it with nourishment, teaching and guidance. So it is when one is delivered from an ungodly soul-tie, some form of Godly soul-tie must take its place, someone within the Body to offer the nourishment and guidance that may be needed on a human level.

To oversimplify the situation, if a person has no Godly social contacts, and just one evil soul-tie, when delivered he should pray for the replacing of that soul-tie with a godly soul-tie.

☞ **Clearly the number-one soul-tie that a Christian must establish, or maintain, is with the Lord Jesus Christ.**

We all lived in darkness and sin until God's light dawned upon us. Thus, we all started out with damaged souls, impaired souls which have been in Satan's kingdom and in the kingdom of darkness. Thus, we are all in need of restoration through Jesus' ministry of restoration for our souls.

Satan is the roaring lion, seeking believers, whom he may devour, and whose souls he desires to rend and tear. That our souls require restoration is seen from the ministry committed to the Son of God, as the Good Shepherd:

> **He restoreth my soul:** he leadeth me in the paths of righteousness for his name's sake.
>
> Ps. 23:3

Jesus restores our souls by leading us into the paths of righteousness, away from the paths of destruction that we have either chosen for ourselves (i.e. "there is a way which seemeth right unto a man, but the end thereof are the ways of death" [Prov. 14:12]), or have been lured into by the agents of the enemy (such as harlots, evil companions, or others seeking to divert us from the paths of God).

May your testimony be like David's glorious testimony of deliverance:

> **Our soul is escaped as a bird out of the snare** of the fowlers: the snare is broken [by deliverance and by the introduction of truth], and **we are escaped.**
>
> Ps. 124:7 [Brackets Ours]

Recommended for Additional Study

ON RELATIONSHIPS:

Cloud, Dr. Henry & Townsend, Dr. Jo
> *Boundaries (When To Say Yes; When To Say No; To Take Control of Your Life)*

Hammond, Frank
> *Soul Ties (Booklet)*

ON CURSES:

Hammond, Frank
> *Breaking of Curses*

Prince, Derek
> *Blessing or Curse*

ON DELIVERANCE

Banks, Bill
> *Deliverance for Children & Teens*
> *Deliverance from Fat & Eating Disorders*
> *Ministering to Abortion's Aftermath*
> *Power for Deliverance: Songs of Deliverance*

Basham, Don
> *Can A Christian Have A Demon?*
> *Deliver Us from Evil*

Hammond, Frank
> *Demons & Deliverance*
> *Kingdom Living for the Famity*
> *Overcoming Rejection*
> *Pigs in the Parlor*

ON THE HOLY SPIRIT & POWER

Banks, Bill
> *Alive Again!*
> *How to Tap into the Wisdom of God*

Bennett, Dennis
> *The Holy Spirit and You*

APPENDIX

The following letter was received from a young mother about a week after receiving deliverance from very strong soul-ties and eight multiple personalities.

March 7, 1997

Mr. Banks:

I wanted to take this opportunity to thank you for your kindness and willingness to minister to myself and to my son. When I first read your books, I thought "there is no one this non-judgmental, not really." I was wrong, Mr. Banks. You show more Christ-like compassion than most ministers. Not just "lip-service," but walking it out. Thank you for showing me there are real people who really care. I pray I can show that type of compassion in my life toward others, including my family.

As far as my deliverance from so much... praise God! I have never felt such freedom, peace, and hope. My husband didn't care that I couldn't explain it as I wanted... he just knows there has been liberty given to me by the grace of God and the cross of Jesus! And we both have more hope for Andy. What some doctors may not realize is, some parents don't give up! There is Jesus Christ, our Healer, and I know He will heal Andy. Andy is really looking forward to meeting you and to have the "bad angels" not bother him.

To give you feedback on significant things you could not have known on your own (because I didn't realize it myself), God reached further to deliver me than I even knew possible. I remember you praying against "rejection from the womb" regarding myself, and my mind went "No," but at the same time I felt something inside react. Then I realized that it was true. Physically, my mother gave birth to me during her seventh month of pregnancy. Emotionally, spiritually my parents wanted me to be a boy; so much so they didn't even pick out a girl's name.

The way I got my name is, I had a "great-uncle" who was a minister who told my parents I was going to be a girl and he wanted to name me. They laughed and told him "sure." His reaction was, since we were at the Dallas airport and he was leaving on Dallas Air, they could just name me "Dallas." I was born, they had no other name, and the joke backfired on me. I was given the name Dallas.

BUT, my Bible says that God has called me by my name, and I am His! In Psalm 139 it says, "While I was still in my mother's womb, You knew me"!!! In God's eyes I am not a joke, or a mistake, or the wrong gender. I am just right!!! I do have a purpose! He wanted me here, and to think of that love... I'm so blessed to KNOW He really does love me. He really does!

I have life, and I have purpose, and I am not rejected.

What a wonderful combination! It's O.K. to be myself. It's O.K. to feel attractive, especially to my husband. It's great to be female!

You mentioned breaking "soul-ties" with those who had abused me, or with whom I had committed sin. I understand that in my spirit. I didn't, until I was set free from those ties. I was in bondage to each one of those people and not able to freely be spiritually joined in every way to my husband. Those other ties were holding me back! I abhor thoughts that used to torment my mind and even my dreams. I desire to be only with my husband. I no longer have any interest in anything pornographic. And I do not refuse my husband's advances as I used to. What a wonderful husband! What a loving Father God is! He set me free to be a real wife! No bad dreams or suggestive ones. No seeking to meet such needs myself, for myself. Sex is like a present from God. I understand that. Pure, no shame, no guilt.

I remember while we were doing the "housecleaning" during deliverance, one named "asthma" coming out. I didn't know there was such a thing as a spirit of asthma! This I can tell you... I've not had to use an inhaler in two days! Praise God! There have been two times when I felt as though an "attack" was about to happen and I said, "No, that thing went and I don't have asthma! In Jesus Name!" And, my breathing was fine!

I also remember losing a spirit named "Coach" and it was the one that told me what to do. I had had a lot of confusion in my mind, and I had a hard time with all kinds of internal thoughts. What was what? Was the Lord speaking to me, or was it myself? And then the thoughts would just become almost deafening. This wasn't anything I had thought about or put on my list. In retrospect, I suspect "Coach" was a spirit sent to confuse me, to keep me from hearing the voice of the Good Shepherd clearly. I no longer have that noise in my head at all! Clear, even thoughts. Thank You, Jesus!

There was one that left that wanted to kill... there were little things that used to set me off. A car driving on my bumper, or Andy (my son) just coming to me to ask a question. I'd react very angrily, then quickly hug him and apologize for yelling at him. Now, driving is no big deal. I enjoy Andy coming to me and wanting a hug, or asking a question (unless he is being mischievous).

I don't fully know all that is happening with me other than to say God has released me from a lot of bondage!

Thank you for being willing to pray for Andy, when others were not. I know God will bless you mightily for all the people you've ministered to! I took forward to seeing Andy delivered and to give you back a praise report! (AGAIN!)

In Jesus,

Dallas, George, and Andy Pines

Praise be to God for His indescribable gift!

For more information on Bill Banks' Books & CD Audio Titles, and for a list of more than 2000 titles on Deliverance, Healing and the Holy Spirit, please visit our website:

www.impactchristianbooks.com

Impact Christian Books is committed to helping families find Christ-centered products, with Godly values, to impact young lives. In line with that goal, we offer over 500 Books, CDs, and DVDs for children & teens at:

www.impactchristiankids.com

www.impactchristianteens.com

Other Titles
by Bill & Sue Banks

Books - Deliverance

Power for Deliverance	$9.95
Deliverance from Fat & Eating Disorders	$7.95
Deliverance for Children & Teens	$9.95
Deliverance from Childlessness	$9.95
Shame Free	$7.95
Ministering to Abortion's Aftermath	$7.95
The Little Skunk (for Children)	$10.99

Books - Healing

Alive Again!	$6.95
Three Kinds of Faith for Healing	$8.95
Overcoming Blocks to Healing	$9.99

Books - The Wisdom of God

How to Tap Into the Wisdom of God	$10.95
The Heavens Declare	$8.95
A Skeptic Discovers Angels are Real	$8.95

Compact Discs (Audio Series)

Salvation & Baptism in the Holy Spirit (1 CD)	$7.00
How I Was Healed of Cancer (1 CD)	$7.00
Deliverance: Setting the Captives Free (11 CDs)	$24.95
Healing is for Today! (14 CDs)	$24.95
AUDIO BOOK: Alive Again (3 CDs)	$19.95
The Baptism in the Holy Spirit (7 CDs)	$19.95
Spiritual Warfare (7 CDs)	$19.95
The Overcoming Power of Prayer (9 CDs)	$24.95
The Gifts of the Spirit (6 CDs)	$19.95
The Heavens Declare (13 CDs)	$24.95
Reincarnation: The Bible's Answer (3 CDs)	$14.95

* 2011 Prices - Subject to Change

Help for Ministering to Children

Deliverance for Children & Teens
by Bill Banks

A practical handbook for ministering deliverance to children. The material in this book is arranged to help parents diagnose their children's problems and find solutions for destructive behavior. Includes a discussion of generational or hereditary issues, the role of discipline in the home, ministering to adopted children, and help for teens.

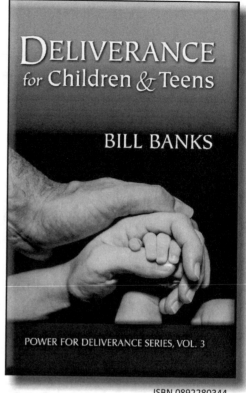

ISBN 0892280344

COMPACT DISC:
Instructions on Deliverance for Children (5-11)
by Derek Prince

Evil is a reality, and Satan preys on the most vulnerable. Rather than being frightened by these facts, parents can take action and learn how to protect and, if necessary, deliver their children from demonic strongholds.The all-important difference becomes clear as we discover our areas of function and responsibility.

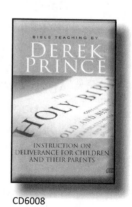

CD6008

Impact Christian Books
www.impactchristianbooks.com
1-800-451-2708

CHILDHOOD TRAUMA

Traumatic experiences in early life, beginning as early as the womb but occurring any time within the vulnerable period of childhood, can provide the door for the *opportunistic enemy* to gain entry. The child or older individual can receive a wound in the realm of his soul by being:

a.) the victim of a wrongful, harmful action of someone else, either intentional, or unintentional

b.) the victim of harm caused by his own action of sinning, either a conscious willful sin or a sin of ignorance

c.) the victim of unpleasant, or cruel circumstances beyond his control

TRAUMA AT BIRTH

The child's need for deliverance may be the result of accidents and associated trauma connected with the birth process, causing impairment or crippling, accidents removing his parents from the scene, as by death in an auto accident, or other such unfortunate occurrences.

These circumstances are in no way related to the sin of the individual child nor the parents of the child. Such tragedies do occur irrespective of the merit of the individuals and are not to be interpreted as punishment, as Scripture clearly teaches:

> "And Jesus answering said unto them, Suppose ye that these Galileans were sinners above all the Galileans, because they suffered such things? I tell you, Nay: but, except ye repent, ye shall all likewise perish. Or those eighteen, upon whom the tower in Siloam fell, and slew them, think ye that they were sinners above all men that dwelt in Jerusalem?" (Luke 13:2-4)

> "And as Jesus passed by, he saw a man which was blind from his birth. And his disciples asked him, saying, Master, who did sin, this man, or his parents, that he was born blind?
>
> Jesus answered, Neither hath this man sinned, nor his parents: but that the works of God should be made manifest in him." (John 9:1-3)

Thus, we observe in the words of the Master Himself, that accidents do occur without the victim having brought the tragedy upon himself by sinning. Such tragedies should serve as a motivation to all to get right with God, and to be prepared to seek the Lord. Jesus healed every person who came to Him seeking deliverance or healing. He turned no one away, either because of the quantity or quality of their sins. None had sinned too greatly to be forgiven or to be ministered to.

These truths are especially important as they are faith-building and offer encouragement to those of us seeking either deliverance or healing. In particular, we do not have to merit the blessing of the Lord's ministry, nor do we have to attain sinless perfection in order to be eligible for it.

DELIVERANCE FOR SALLY FROM "IT"

Sally, a young nurse from our fellowship, phoned one day to ask if my wife and I would pray with her.

"I know that I need further deliverance. I don't have any idea what it is I'm up against this time, but I'm sure it isn't rejection because we've already dealt with that and I really believe that it is gone. This is something that is similar to rejection," she said thoughtfully.

"I know that I'm saved and that the Lord loves me, and that I've been baptized in the Spirit and walking with Him for over five years, but there is still something tormenting me."

I reflected upon the previous ministry with Sally. She had been adopted when only a few days old by an older couple who had lovingly raised her. Having been raised in a home as an only child by older parents and knowing that she had been adopted, Sally had battled rejection and abandonment problems. She had been delivered of both spirits about six months earlier and had also forgiven her birth-mother for abandoning her.

"It's embarrassing to talk about, but I'm sure most girls, or women, think of themselves as female; as a 'she' or a 'her.' For some reason, I always think of myself as an 'it.' I really don't understand why, but that's always been the way that I've thought of myself. I'm almost thirty years old, and all the dates I've had in my life you could count on one hand. I'm not upset about it because I've had no desire to date either."

I recalled that we had always known Sally to be a friendly, outgoing, loving, patient, and compassionate Christian. We had observed that although she was very pleasant and people genuinely liked her, she did not date. In spite of the fact that she had a great personality, Sally seemed to have no desire to date and did not seem, upon reflection, to be particularly feminine. She always dressed neatly but not in a very feminine way, almost like a tomboy, usually wearing a typical pantsuit and her hair close-cropped.

This certainly sounded abnormal, unnatural - probably demonic. However, being totally in the dark as to what we were up against, I suggested that we pray and ask God to intervene. We prayed a simple prayer, something to this effect: "Lord Jesus, we acknowledge that You are the Deliverer. It is Your ministry and we know that You know all about Sally's problems and You want her whole even more than we do. In Your name we command this thing tormenting her to identify itself and to come out of her ."

Then we just waited ....

Sally began to shake and shiver. It was evident to us that the Lord was doing something and that she was apparently seeing something. Therefore we decided to simply wait and let the Lord finish His sovereign ministry to her.

A few minutes later she looked up, her eyes wet with tears, and said, "Wow! You won't believe what the Lord just showed me. I was in a large white room and I began to be able to see details. You know I'm a nurse, so I instantly recognized the scene as a hospital delivery room. I could see the clock on the wall. I could see the delivery room staff milling around. I could hear everything they said. I knew everything going on in that room. It was amazing to me, and then I noticed that there was a woman on the table who had obviously just given birth."

Sally paused briefly for a breath and continued her description of what she'd seen. "And, suddenly, I felt myself being carried from the corner where I was, out toward the center of the room, and I realized with a start that I was the new-born baby! The nurse carrying me attempted to hand me to the new mother. She took one look at me with a sneer on her face, put up a hand to stop the nurse and snarled, 'Get IT out of here!'"

She sighed deeply and we all then realized that the curse of being an "it" had, in essence, been laid upon her from the moment of her birth. As a result of her being unwanted by her mother and put up for adoption, she had not only picked up the spirit of rejection and the spirit of abandonment from which she had previously been delivered, but also this unusual and peculiar spirit which had caused her to think of herself as an "it." We then prayed again with her, breaking the curse of being an "it" and cast out the spirit which made her think of herself as "it." This peculiar spirit was no doubt a member of the *self-rejection* family or grouping of spirits.

After she was delivered, Sally asked that we pray with her that she might be able to start dating, "preferably a Spirit-filled man." Within a week she was back to say "You won't believe this. I can scarcely believe it, myself, but the Lord has answered that prayer. Would you believe, I have been dating a Spirit-filled man, and he has asked me to marry him!" As it turned out, Sally didn't marry him, but it was a bold move in a new direction for her, and it blessed us all to see the how far "beyond our ability to think or ask" the Lord could do.

Trauma From The Womb

Sally's story is an example of how early in the life of an infant problems can enter, from the very moment of birth. To go a step further, in certain cases a spirit or spirits can gain entry even before birth. This is a difficult concept, and seems totally unfair to us. Before looking at two ways in which it can happen, let us first consider a Scriptural example. The Bible records that John the Baptist, whose age was birth minus three months and who was thus in the womb of his mother, was filled with the Holy Spirit. If a child in the womb has the capacity to receive the Holy Spirit, then it is certainly logical that a child in the womb has the capacity to receive an evil spirit.

There are two main routes by which an evil spirit can gain entry to a fetus. First, and most common, is the root of inheritance. Second, is through trauma or fear experienced by the mother. The second could be termed to be inherited, although we normally consider inheritance to include only those conditions overtly manifested in the mother, father or ancestors. However, from a spiritual standpoint, the seeds or roots that give legal right of entry to a demon may have been planted in the womb, or even a generation or even several generations earlier.

The concept of a child being demonized is particularly offensive to us, because it is especially unfair for an innocent, defenseless child to be vulnerable to demonic invasion. However, it is unfortunately in line with the character of Satan, an opportunistic enemy, to mount an attack upon the weakest and most defenseless victims.

In many cases, the demonic attack on an infant's personality or well-being is not based on the actions of parents. However, if we consider the extreme cases where neglect is involved, such as in light of the situation of drug-addicted parents, it becomes more understandable how infants can be targeted. Drug-addicted parents give birth to drug-addicted babies. This is not unfair upon the part of God; it is simply an outworking of the law of cause and effect. Similarly, the prospective parent who goes to a séance while pregnant, can be exposing the as yet unborn child to Satanic influences and contagion. This can hold true even for a child not yet conceived.

There is another possible explanation for a child having a demonic problem, and that is the outworking of a curse. If a great-grandmother, for example, practiced witchcraft, we may see the results of her sin of being a "hater of God" manifested in her offspring to the fourth generation (Exodus 20:5).

Trauma in Early Childhood

Many (probably most) spirits enter individuals as infants or children, and of course adults can acquire demonic issues later in life. Children, I believe, are the most vulnerable, even than infants, because their consciousness is developing along with their minds, wills and their awareness of right and wrong.

The young child is vulnerable to many fears because he does not yet have the natural defensive weapon of a fully developed mind, the means by which an older individual may rationally defend himself. A child, for instance, who is told that the bogeyman will "get him" may pick up a fear because he is unaware that there is no such person, and that the person who mentioned the bogeyman was only joking.

An incident that occurred when I was about twelve illustrates this truth. My parents were taking my five-year-old brother, his good friend, my sister and me on an afternoon outing to visit a commercially developed cave. The five year old friend of my brother, leaned over the front seat and asked, "Where are we going?"

My Dad, who loved to tease and knowing we had not been outside of the Midwest much, said "Well, we're going to Mexico."

My family all laughed, thinking it was a great joke. But we noticed a few moments later that the guest was sobbing quietly in the back seat with tears running down his cheeks. In spite of a good time at the caverns, and an atoning treat of ice cream cones, our guest didn't really relax until we returned him to his parents.

Even totally innocent teasing, or joking, can cause problems for children who, because of their immaturity, have difficulty distinguishing between reality and unreality, truth and fiction. Thus, parents should be careful of joking or teasing with their children, and make sure that the child knows what is a joke. When fishing with your children, a simple joshing statement such as, "Be good (an unspecific, impossible goal) or I'll use you for bait," could cause harm if the child believes you mean it. For more information, refer to the "Teasing" section under Gates of Abuse.

Trauma through Encounters with Death

It is very difficult for a child to grasp the concept of, or to cope with the realities of, death. This is especially true when it involves a loved one.

The Death, or Near-Death, of a Parent

We encountered a doorway involving a variation of the fear of death in our own family. I was a terminal cancer patient in 1970 when my oldest son, Kevin, was about three and a half. I was hospitalized for several months, prior to being healed sovereignly by the Lord. He visited me at the hospital before I came home, and was very loving and affectionate. The day I returned home, he gave me a good hug, a "big love," and said "Hi Dad, sure glad you're home. Glad to see you," and went out to play.

We thought my younger son, Steve, at one-and-a-half, hadn't really been old enough to grasp any of the gravity of the situation. When I returned home, however, he crawled up into my lap. He put his arms around my neck, and hung on for all he was worth for at least forty-five minutes, which a returning father didn't mind at all. However, it did show us that my illness and absence from the home had made a far greater impression on his little mind or spirit than we had imagined.

We made the assumption that Kevin had taken it in stride. However, when he was about eleven, we noticed a change in his personality. All of a sudden, he was no longer able to receive affection from me. He would get very giddy and silly when I was around him. I first noticed it manifesting one night when I went into the boys' bedroom to say prayers with them. He wouldn't let me kiss him goodnight.

He could receive affection from his mother and other relatives. He was loving toward me at other times, but particularly at night, when I prayed with him and tried to kiss him before bed, he was not able to receive it.

It was certainly peculiar and we realized that this was symptomatic of something deeper, although we weren't sure just what. Since we weren't able to get a handle on it or to resolve it any other way, we decided to try a rather natural technique of having me simply spend extra time alone with him. I set aside a half hour every evening to spend just with him playing ping-pong, cards, or whatever he wanted to do. I just wanted to have some quality time with him.

After about two or three months, one night when I went in to say prayers with him, he prayed a prayer that caused my jaw to drop, tears to fill my eyes, and a light of understanding to dawn. His prayer went something like this, "Dear Jesus, thank you for not letting my Daddy die."

Here, once again, our assumptions had been incorrect. There had been a far deeper wound to his spirit due to my absence and illness than we had imagined. Because of this wound to his spirit, a fear had entered. It was an unspeakable fear, so deep and so great that he had been unable to face it or to articulate it. It was the fear that he would lose his father through death. After he prayed that short prayer that night, he was set free from this lingering torment. From that time on he was able to both receive and give normal, healthy affection toward me. The power of love and trust had broken through the barrier of fear, and allowed God's light to bear upon this area of darkness; and it had brought deliverance.

Deliverance for Children & Teens
by Bill Banks

A practical handbook for ministering deliverance to children. The material in this book is arranged to help parents diagnose their children's problems and find solutions for destructive behavior. Includes a discussion of generational or hereditary issues, the role of discipline in the home, ministering to adopted children, and help for teens.

Impact Christian Books
www.impactchristianbooks.com
1-800-451-2708

DELIVERANCE
for Children & Teens

BILL BANKS

POWER FOR DELIVERANCE SERIES, VOL. 3

Children's Books

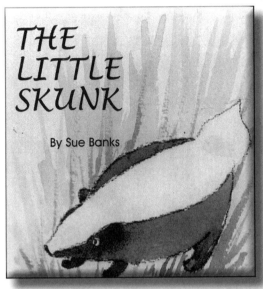

ISBN 0892281200

The Little Skunk
by Sue Banks

A children's book on deliverance! For the child to read with a parent to understand the subject of deliverance without fear. (Deliverance need not be frightening if properly presented).

Includes color illustrations to accompany the story, and assistance at the end for the parent to pray with the child. Watch how Charlie, Billy and Susie try to get the little skunk out of their house!

My Own Psalm 91
by Peggy Joyce Ruth

My Own Psalm 91 Book introduces your child to the value of an intimate relationship with God and the importance of prayer. The images in this book portray a compelling visual and an easy to understand presentation of Psalm 91 for young minds.

Help your child experience this powerful psalm at an early age and learn how to overcome fear!

ISBN 0892281200

For over 400 Children's Books, CDs, DVDs, Visit us online at

www.impactchristiankids.com

An Introduction to
Deliverance!

ISBN 089228031X

Power for Deliverance (Songs of Deliverance)
by Bill & Sue Banks

From over 30 years of counseling and ministering deliverance, Bill Banks highlights the common root causes of emotional and mental torment, and walks the reader through steps to be set free. Includes revelations from over a dozen people delivered from various trauma and torment.

This book shows that there is help for oppressed, tormented and compulsive people, and that the solution is as old as the ministry of Jesus Christ!

Impact Christian Books
www.impactchristianbooks.com
1-800-451-2708

Deliverance from

Fat & Eating Disorders

DELIVERANCE FROM FAT
& EATING DISORDERS

POWER
FOR
DELIVERANCE

EAT

BILL BANKS

FOREWORD BY DR. FREDERIC PFEIFFER

ISBN 0892280328

Deliverance from Fat & Eating Disorders
by Bill Banks

Powerful help for those who have been unable to lose weight. Learn about unnatural weight gain, and common spiritual roots.

This book reveals dozens of spiritual reasons for unnatural weight gain, as well as eating disorders like Bulimia, Anorexia, Obesity and more. Included are fifteen testimonies of people who found freedom from the bondage of excess weight!

Impact Christian Books
www.impactchristianbooks.com
1-800-451-2708

What Are the True Effects of
Abortion?

Have you had an abortion?
Do you carry guilt or fear inside due to this experience?
Could miscarriage or infertility be rooted in past abortions?
Does Jesus yearn to deliver all who are in bondage?
Are you free to be all that God intended you to be?

ISBN 0892280573

Ministering to Abortion's Aftermath
by Bill & Sue Banks

Millions of women have had abortions. Many were unaware of the phyiscal, emotional and spiritual consequences, and still carry the trauma of the event with them - even in later years.

In Ministering to Abortion's Aftermath, read a dozen real-life stories of women who have found deliverance and freedom from the various bondages associated with abortion, including emotional torment, physical complications, and more. Learn how their triumph can be yours.

Discover the strategic steps and simple truths that have led these women, and hundreds more like them, to be set free. This book is full of hope - *hope that heals*!

Impact Christian Books
www.impactchristianbooks.com
1-800-451-2708

Deliverance from
Infertility

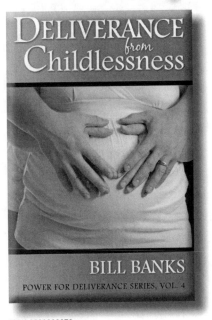

ISBN 0892280379

Deliverance from Childlessness
by Bill Banks

Are you aware that demonic spirits can prevent childbirth? Or that the Bible has a lot to say about childlessness?

This book ministers to women and men with truths to overcome barrenness. Learn how curses of childlessness come into being and how they may be broken; and learn ways that spirits of infertility and sterility enter and how to cast them out.

Read 6 testimonies of couples who were infertile and who now have children!

Impact Christian Books
www.impactchristianbooks.com
1-800-451-2708

Defeat the Root Spirit of
SHAME!

ISBN 0892280913

Shame Free
by Bill & Sue Banks

Sabotaged By Shame, Now Saved From Shame...

* Has shame maimed you?

* Have you been crippled by embarassment?

* Do you stress about the opinion of others?

* Do you have a fear of speaking in public?

Shame has been found to be a root spirit that affects individuals from earliest childhood. It has also been found to be bad fruit that may plague individuals throughout their lives. Discover how you, or someone you know, may live Shame Free.

0892280913 *Paperback*

Impact Christian Books
www.impactchristianbooks.com
1-800-451-2708

Keys to Unlock
Bible Prophecy

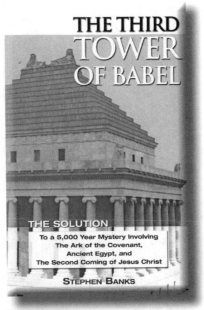

THE THIRD
TOWER
OF BABEL

THE SOLUTION

To a 5,000 Year Mystery Involving
The Ark of the Covenant,
Ancient Egypt, and
The Second Coming of Jesus Christ

STEPHEN BANKS

ISBN 0892280980

The Third Tower of Babel
by Stephen Banks

The most exalted image of Jesus Christ, the symbol of His Second Coming, has been overlooked during centuries of biblical research. Now, from the pages of Zechariah, Isaiah, and Daniel, this remarkable symbol of the Messiah is revealed.

Through this symbol of Jesus Christ you will find the key to unlock a 5000 year mystery involving the Ark of the Covenant, the coming New World Order, and the Second Coming of Jesus Christ.

Impact Christian Books
www.impactchristianbooks.com
1-800-451-2708

A Miraculous Healing from
Cancer

Alive Again!

**Bill Banks:
Terminal Cancer:
48 hours to live.
Miraculously
healed!**

ISBN 0892280484

Alive Again!
by Bill Banks

One of the greatest healing testimonies in print. A healing from cancer lasting over 30 years.

With six different terminal conditions, and numerous malignant tumors, read how one man sought the healing accounts in Scripture for strength and encouragement. Follow his story as he fights to live during 6 months of chemotherapy, radiation, and dialysis, and then is told he has only 48 hours to live! When the doctors gave up - God didn't. Find answers to the questions: Is it God's will to heal? And, does God want to heal you?

Impact Christian Books
www.impactchristianbooks.com
1-800-451-2708

~v-√v—√v- **From 30 years in the**

Healing Ministry...

...comes answers to questions such as:

Is it God's will to heal?

Are there blocks to physical healing?

What about Paul's Thorn?

Have you considered Job?

Does Jesus yearn to deliver all who are in bondage?

ISBN 0892281367

Overcoming Blocks to Healing
by Bill & Sue Banks

One of the most important books on healing and the healing ministry to reach the Church! From 30 years of ministering in hospitals, churches, and homes, Bill Banks explains why some people are not healed, and what they can do about it.

Has Jesus changed His mind, or are there blocks to healing as a part of Satan's strategy to keep us sick? Find answers to over 30 questions about God's willingness to heal.

The Classic Guide to
Deliverance

ISBN 0892280271

ISBN 0892281995

Pigs in the Parlor
by Frank Hammond

A handbook for deliverance from demons and spiritual oppression. Frank Hammond explains the practical application of the ministry of deliverance, patterned after the ministry of Jesus Christ.

Frank Hammond presents information on such topics as:
* How demons enter, * When deliverance is needed, * Seven steps in receiving & ministering deliverance, * Seven steps in maintaining deliverance, * Self deliverance, * Demon manifestations, * Binding and loosing, * Practical advice for the deliverance minister, * Answers to commonly asked questions, and more.

Study Guide

A companion guide to help you dig deeper into this deliverance classic!

This guide has been designed as a tool to enable you to:
➢ diagnose your own, personal deliverance needs
➢ walk you through the process of becoming free
➢ equip you to set others free from demonic torment

This new Study Guide includes:
♦ Questions and answers on *Pigs in the Parlor* on a chapter by chapter basis.
♦ New information in each chapter to further your knowledge of deliverance.
♦ Powerful scriptures to support the ministry of deliverance
♦ Quotes from early Church fathers on the validity and necessity of casting out demons, and more!

Impact Christian Books
www.impactchristianbooks.com
1-800-451-2708

Other Titles By Frank Hammond

THE BREAKING OF CURSES

The Bible refers to curses over 230 times, and lists 70 sins that cause curses. Frank Hammond provides information on spoken curses, generational curses, cursed objects and most importantly, steps to breaking curses. Learn how curses are just as real today as in biblical times - and how you may deliver yourself and your family from them. "If the Son sets you free, you will be free indeed!"

089228109X *Paperback*

OVERCOMING REJECTION

Learn how to effectively deal with the all-too-common root problem of rejection. Frank Hammond addresses both rejection and the fear of rejection, examines their source and their effects, and provides steps for the reader to be set free!

0892281057 *Paperback*

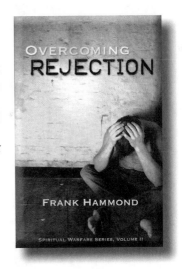

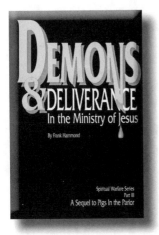

DEMONS & DELIVERANCE

A sequel to Pigs in the Parlor. This book sets forth guiding principles from Scripture and the ministry of Jesus Christ for confronting demons and delivering the oppressed. Learn more about the believer's commission and authority to confront and drive out evil spirits.

0892280018 *Paperback*

Impact Christian Books
www.impactchristianbooks.com
1-800-451-2708

Impact Christian Books

These books are available through your local bookstore,
or you may order directly from
Impact Christian Books.

Website: www.impactchristianbooks.com

Phone Order Line: **1-800-451-2708**
(314)-822-3309

Address: **Impact Christian Books**
332 Leffingwell Ave. Suite #101
Kirkwood, MO 63122

- You may also request a Free Catalog -